T0316503

Cambridge Elements

Elements in the Philosophy of Physics
edited by
James Owen Weatherall
University of California, Irvine

FOUNDATIONS OF QUANTUM MECHANICS

Emily Adlam
University of Cambridge

CAMBRIDGE
UNIVERSITY PRESS

CAMBRIDGE
UNIVERSITY PRESS

University Printing House, Cambridge CB2 8BS, United Kingdom

One Liberty Plaza, 20th Floor, New York, NY 10006, USA

477 Williamstown Road, Port Melbourne, VIC 3207, Australia

314–321, 3rd Floor, Plot 3, Splendor Forum, Jasola District Centre,
New Delhi – 110025, India

79 Anson Road, #06–04/06, Singapore 079906

Cambridge University Press is part of the University of Cambridge.

It furthers the University's mission by disseminating knowledge in the pursuit of
education, learning, and research at the highest international levels of excellence.

www.cambridge.org
Information on this title: www.cambridge.org/9781108794442
DOI: 10.1017/9781108885515

© Emily Adlam 2021

First published 2021

A catalogue record for this publication is available from the British Library.

ISBN 978-1-108-79444-2 Paperback
ISSN 2632-413X (online)
ISSN 2632-4121 (print)

Cambridge University Press has no responsibility for the persistence or accuracy of
URLs for external or third-party internet websites referred to in this publication
and does not guarantee that any content on such websites is, or will remain,
accurate or appropriate.

Foundations of Quantum Mechanics

Elements in the Philosophy of Physics

DOI: 10.1017/9781108885515
First published online: February 2021

Emily Adlam
University of Cambridge
Author for correspondence: Emily Adlam, eadlam90@gmail.com

Abstract: Quantum mechanics is an extraordinarily successful scientific theory. But more than 100 years after it was first introduced, the interpretation of the theory remains controversial. This Element introduces some of the most puzzling questions at the foundations of quantum mechanics and provides an up-to-date and forward-looking survey of the most prominent ways in which physicists and philosophers of physics have attempted to resolve them. The topics covered include non-locality, contextuality, the reality of the wavefunction, and measurement problem. The discussion is supplemented with descriptions of some of the most important mathematical results from recent work in quantum foundations, including Bell's theorem, the Kochen-Specker theorem, and the PBR theorem.

Keywords: quantum foundations, philosophy of physics, non-locality, contextuality, Measurement problem

Isbns: 9781108794442 (PB), 9781108885515 (OC)
Issns: 2632-413X (online), 2632-4121 (print)

Contents

1 Introduction

One of the most important goals of physics is to come up with theories which successfully predict observable physical phenomena. But even when a theory is successful in the empirical sense, there remain many questions to be answered. What, if anything, does a successful predictive algorithm tell us about the way the world is? What ontology does the theory suggest? How does the theory relate to other successful physical theories? How does it relate to our own experiences? What does the theory tell us about familiar concepts like space, time, and matter?

In attempting to answer these questions, we are engaging in what is known as foundations of physics. Quantum foundations is the branch of foundations of physics that relates to quantum mechanics, the physical theory developed in the early twentieth century which applies to phenomena at very small scales. While there are certainly interesting foundational problems to be addressed for all of our major physical theories,[1] quantum foundations has attracted an unusual amount of attention because there seems to be something uniquely puzzling about quantum mechanics. Most famously, there exists no consensus about the physical interpretation of the predictive algorithm that quantum mechanics gives us, and many of the alternatives under consideration paint a picture of a physical world which is radically different from the classical world of our pre-quantum imaginings.

Although there is a significant intersection between foundational questions and the traditional domain of philosophy, quantum foundations is distinct from the philosophy of quantum mechanics in that the two fields typically involve different methodological approaches. One of the important innovations made by Bell in proving his famous theorem, which we will discuss in Section 3, was that it is possible to address foundational questions in a *quantitative* way by means of mathematical proof, and subsequently the field of quantum foundations has applied similar quantitative approaches to many other conceptual questions. It is this mathematical approach which makes quantum foundations a branch of physics rather than philosophy – although of course researchers in quantum foundations have many interests in common with their peers in the philosophy of quantum mechanics, and the field can be understood as sitting at the intersection of physics, maths, and philosophy.

Before we go further, we should address head-on the not uncommon view that making empirical predictions is the *only* goal of physics, and that it is

---

[1] For an overview of some interesting problems in the foundations of special and general relativity, see Maudlin (2012); for statistical mechanics, see Sklar (1993); and for classical mechanics, see Sklar (2012).

therefore pointless to worry about interpretations or to ask any of the other conceptual questions with which quantum foundations is concerned. As a first response, we observe that many people with an interest in science are driven not only by the desire to make predictions but also by the desire to understand how the world works, and quantum foundations exists in part to satisfy this intellectual thirst. Of course it is true that we can never be completely certain that the conclusions we reach in this endeavour are correct, but then one can never be completely certain that one's predictive theories are universally correct either.

Furthermore, quantum foundations would be important even if the only purpose of science *were* to make predictions, because thinking deeply about the nature of quantum mechanics and coming to a better understanding of the physical reality from which it arises is likely to lead to progress on outstanding problems in physics. This is particularly important right now because many physicists have come to believe that fundamental physics is in a state of stagnation, with little meaningful progress having been made in the last few decades (Hossenfelder 2018). It seems entirely possible that this has arisen because physicists never properly got to grips with what quantum mechanics tells us about the world, and therefore all subsequent physics has been based on an improper understanding of the earlier theory, leading us into a dead end. Thus quantum foundations is not merely an exercise in intellectual curiosity – it may be the best hope we have of breaking out of the impasse that physics seems to have found itself in. After all, many historic advances in physics have resulted from thinking deeply about conceptual questions; for example, Einstein's theory of special relativity is the result of asking foundational questions about the nature of time and simultaneity (Einstein 1905).

This Element offers a short tour through some important topics in quantum foundations. The next section introduces the basics of quantum mechanics together with some ideas and notation that we will use throughout this Element. Since the motivating principle of quantum foundations is to address conceptual questions with mathematical methods, in Sections 3, 4, and 5 we introduce an important mathematical result from the field and then discuss the conceptual issues linked to it. In Section 6 we give a brief summary of some other areas of quantum foundations that due to considerations of space cannot be covered in detail here. Finally, in the concluding section, we give an assessment of the current state of quantum foundations and make some suggestions about what its future might look like.

2 Preliminaries

2.1 What Is Quantum Mechanics?

Quantum mechanics has its origins in a number of apparently minor problems that puzzled physicists in the late nineteenth and early twentieth centuries. One of these was the 'black-body problem', which was solved by Max Planck in 1900 using the hypothesis that energy is radiated and absorbed in discrete packets known as quanta. Another was the 'photoelectric effect', for which Einstein proposed a similarly quantum solution in 1905. Subsequently, in 1913, Niels Bohr came up with a quantised theory of atomic structure to explain Ernest Rutherford's experimental observations. These early quantum ideas were developed over the first half of the twentieth century by physicists such as Schrödinger, Heisenberg, Born, von Neumann, Dirac, Pauli, Hilbert, and many others, and the theory that emerged has become known as quantum mechanics.[2]

Quantum mechanics is in many ways more a methodological prescription than a concrete scientific theory (Gell-Mann 1980, Nielsen and Chuang 2011), since it sets out a mathematical framework for the construction of physical theories that must be supplemented with detailed experimental work to determine which specific mathematical objects represent the actual physical systems whose behaviour we would like to predict. However, the field of quantum foundations is largely concerned with this abstract structure rather than with any specific realisation of it, and hence for us it is sufficient to regard quantum mechanics as being characterised by the following four postulates (Nielsen and Chuang 2011) (see Strang (2016) for an introduction to the linear algebra terminology used in these postulates):

1. To every physical system we ascribe a Hilbert space, $\mathscr{H}$, known as the state space of the system.[3] At any given time, the system is completely described by its state vector, which is a unit vector $|\psi\rangle$ in the state space.
2. Closed quantum systems evolve by unitary transformations.[4] In particular, a closed quantum system can be associated with a fixed Hermitian operator[5] H, and the time evolution of the state of the system is then given by $H|\psi(t)\rangle = i\hbar \frac{d|\psi(0)\rangle}{dt}$ (i.e., the Schrödinger equation).

---

[2] See Lindley (2008) for an engaging account of the early history of quantum mechanics.

[3] A Hilbert space is a complex vector space equipped with an inner product.

[4] A unitary transformation is a transformation that preserves the value of the inner product; unitary operators U satisfy $U^{\dagger}U = \mathbb{I}$, where $U^{\dagger}$ denotes the conjugate transpose of U and $\mathbb{I}$ denotes the identity operator.

[5] A Hermitian operator is an operator that is equal to its own conjugate transpose.

3. A measurement is described by a projective measurement, which is a Hermitian operator on the state space of the system. The projective measurement can be decomposed into a set of operators $\{P_m\}$ sum to the identity operator, each associated with a measurement outcome. When a system is prepared in the state $|\psi\rangle$ and the measurement $\{P_m\}$ is performed, the probability of obtaining the outcome associated with P_m is equal to $Tr(P_m|\psi\rangle\langle\psi|)$, where $Tr(..)$ denotes the trace and $|\psi\rangle\langle\psi|$ denotes the outer product of the state vector $|\psi\rangle$ with itself; after this result has been obtained, the state of the system is $\frac{P_m|\psi\rangle}{\sqrt{Tr(P_m|\psi\rangle\langle\psi|)}}$.

4. When we combine two physical systems, the state space for the resulting composite system is the tensor product of the individual state spaces; if we combine n systems prepared in states $|\psi_1\rangle, |\psi_2\rangle, \ldots, |\psi_n\rangle$, the resulting joint state is $|\psi_1\rangle \otimes |\psi_2\rangle \otimes \ldots \otimes |\psi_n\rangle$.

2.1.1 Quantum States

Let's consider an example. Take a quantum system with a Hilbert space of dimension two, such as a particle that can have spin pointing up or down. We will write the state 'spin up' as the vector $\begin{bmatrix} 1 \\ 0 \end{bmatrix}$ or equivalently the ket $|0\rangle$ and the state 'spin down' as the vector $\begin{bmatrix} 0 \\ 1 \end{bmatrix}$ or equivalently $|1\rangle$. The inner product of the vectors $|\psi\rangle$ and $|\phi\rangle$, written as $\langle\phi|\psi\rangle$, is given by multiplying each entry in $|\psi\rangle$ by the conjugate transpose of the corresponding entry in $|\phi\rangle$, so for example we have $\langle 0|1\rangle = 1 \times 0 + 0 \times 1 = 0$. By convention, quantum states are normalised so that for any state $|\psi\rangle$, $\langle\psi|\psi\rangle = 1$.

Suppose we apply some measurement $M = \{P_0, P_1\}$ to the system when it is in state $|0\rangle$. The measurement operators P_0 and P_1 are both represented by 2×2 matrices. One possible measurement we can perform on this system is a spin measurement, where the operator $P_0 = |0\rangle\langle 0|$ is associated with the property 'spin up' and the operator $P_1 = |1\rangle\langle 1|$ is associated with the property 'spin down'. If we perform this measurement when the system is in state $|0\rangle$, the probability of obtaining the outcome 'spin up' is $Tr(P_0|0\rangle\langle 0|)$, which can be rearranged to $\langle 0|P_0|0\rangle = \langle 0|0\rangle\langle 0|0\rangle$ which equals 1 due to the normalisation of quantum states. So the probability of obtaining the outcome 'spin up' when the system is in the state 'spin up' is equal to 1, and a similar calculation shows that the probability of obtaining the outcome 'spin down' when the system is in the state 'spin down' is equal to 1, exactly as we would expect.

Now if this were a classical system, then spin up and spin down would be the only possibilities for the state. But because this is a quantum system, the state can also be a vector like $\begin{bmatrix} \frac{1}{\sqrt{2}} \\ \frac{1}{\sqrt{2}} \end{bmatrix}$ or, in quantum-mechanical notation,

$\frac{1}{\sqrt{2}}(|0\rangle + |1\rangle)$. In this state, the particle's spin is neither up nor down; it is an equal superposition of both, and when we measure its spin the probability of getting a 'spin up' result is $Tr(P_0 \frac{1}{\sqrt{2}}(|0\rangle + |1\rangle)\frac{1}{\sqrt{2}}(\langle 0| + \langle 1|))$, which comes out to 0.5. That is, we have a 50 per cent chance of getting the result up and a 50 per cent chance of getting the result down. Superpositions like this allow a continuous range of states between 'spin up' and 'spin down'. Note that by applying the formula in postulate three, we find that after the result 'spin up' is obtained, the system will always be in the state $|0\rangle$, which corresponds to 'spin up', so even if the particle did not have a definite state of spin before the measurement, after the measurement it is in the 'spin up' state corresponding to the observed measurement outcome.

If this were a classical system, then we would always be able to find out its state with certainty, provided we were able to perform sufficiently sensitive measurements. But in quantum mechanics, this is no longer true. That is, given two arbitrary quantum states ψ_1, ψ_2, it will not always be possible to find a measurement $\{M_1, M_2\}$ such that if we perform this measurement when the system is in state ψ_1, we are guaranteed to get outcome M_1, and if we perform the measurement when the system is in state ψ_2, we are guaranteed to get outcome M_2. Usually, the best we will be able to do is to come up with a measurement $\{M_1, M_2\}$ such that if we perform this measurement when the system is in state ψ_1, we get outcome M_1 with some probability p_1, and if we perform this measurement when the system is in state ψ_2, we get outcome M_1 with probability $p_2 < p_1$. Thus, when we do perform the measurement and get outcome M_1, we will be able to conclude that it is more likely the state was ψ_1 rather than ψ_2.

However, there are certain sets of states for which it is possible to find distinguishing measurements. In particular, this is the case for any set of states that are all orthogonal to each other, where we say two states $|a\rangle$ and $|b\rangle$ are orthogonal if their inner product is zero, i.e. $\langle a|b \rangle = 0$. In real vector spaces with two or three dimensions, 'orthogonal' means the same as 'perpendicular', and in other vector spaces, it can be thought of as a generalisation of that notion. The states $|0\rangle$ and $|1\rangle$ in our example are orthogonal, since $\langle 0|1 \rangle = 0$, and indeed they can be perfectly distinguished by the spin measurement $\{P_0, P_1\}$, since we will always get the outcome 'spin up' when the system is in state $|0\rangle$ and we will always get the outcome 'spin down' when the system is in state $|1\rangle$.

The fact that quantum states in general cannot be perfectly distinguished poses obvious practical challenges when it comes to performing and analysing quantum experiments, since it means we must draw our conclusions from the statistical ensemble of the results over a large number of experiments, rather than the result of any individual experiment. This is also a first indication that quantum states may have properties quite unlike classical states, and in forthcoming sections we will see that this is borne out in a variety of interesting ways.

2.1.2 Mixed States and Density Operators

On the face of it, the postulates we have set out suggest that the state of a quantum system must always be describable by a state vector in some Hilbert space. But, in fact, there are two ways in which we can obtain different types of states within this formalism. First, we can select a state from among a set of states $\{|\psi_i\rangle\}$ with some set of probabilities $\{p(\psi_i)\}$, giving rise to a probabilistic mixture $\rho = \sum_i p(\psi_i)|\psi_i\rangle\langle\psi_i|$; this is known as a proper mixture (d' Espagnat 1971, Busch et al. 1996). Second, we can take two systems A, B in an entangled state ψ (see Section 3) and then throw away the information about the state of A, leaving B in a reduced state $\rho = Tr_A(|\psi\rangle\langle\psi|)$; this is known as an improper mixture (d' Espagnat 1971, Busch et al. 1996). Happily, it turns out that these two methods of preparation give rise to exactly the same type of mathematical object – to wit, a density matrix, a positive Hermitian matrix of trace one. States that can be represented as state vectors are known as 'pure states', and these states can also be represented as density matrices, since the state vector $|\psi\rangle$ corresponds to the density matrix $|\psi\rangle\langle\psi|$, whereas states that can only be written as density matrices and have no state vector representation are known as 'mixed states'.

From the original four postulates set out in Section 2.1, we can derive statements about the behaviour of density matrices. The set of possible evolutions is expanded to include all evolutions that can be obtained by appending some other system to the original system and then applying a unitary evolution as described in postulate two to the whole, which leads to the set of all completely positive trace-preserving (CPTP) maps[6]; the set of possible measurements is expanded to include all measurements that can be implemented by appending an extra system to the original system and applying a projective measurement as defined in postulate three to the whole, which leads to the set of all positive operator valued measures (POVMs). A POVM is a set of positive semi-definite

---

[6] A completely positive trace-preserving map is an operator which does not change the trace of the matrices that it acts on (this is the 'trace-preserving' property), such that if we take the tensor product of this operator with the identity matrix and apply the result to a positive semi-definite matrix, the resulting matrix will still be a positive semi-definite (this is the 'completely positive' property).

operators[7] $\{K_n\}$ that sum to the identity operator; the probability of obtaining the result associated with the operator K_n when we the measured system has density matrix ρ is given by $Tr(K_n\rho)$, which is similar to the corresponding formula for a projective measurement. In postulate three, we were also able to give a formula for the state that a system will be in after a projective measurement, but unfortunately, this cannot be done for POVMs, because any given POVM can be implemented in a number of different ways and the post-measurement state depends on the particular implementation (Nielsen and Chuang 2011, Paris 2012, Landau and Lifshitz 2013). In fact, this is true of projective measurements as well (for example, sometimes in a projective measurement the state being measured is destroyed!), but postulate three provides a simple, natural update rule that works in most situations and is widely accepted as canonical. By contrast, for POVMs there is no such simple, canonical approach.

It should be noted that since the ideal of pure states, unitary operators, and projective measurements can seldom be perfectly realised in the laboratory, in real applications we are mostly dealing with mixed states, CPTP maps, and POVMs, rather than pure states, unitary transformations, and projective measurements (de Muynck 2007).

We pause at this point to reinforce that the pedagogical approach of deriving the existence of density matrices, CPTP maps, and POVMs from the four postulates set out in Section 2.1 – an approach known as the 'Church of the Larger Hilbert Space', (Timpson 2008) – is not entirely uncontroversial. There are also advocates of the 'Church of the Smaller Hilbert Space' who contend that the density matrix should be thought of as the fundamental object of quantum mechanics and that we have no reason to suppose that quantum systems cannot be in mixed states without being derived from either a larger pure state or a probabilistic mixture of pure states (Dürr et al. 2005, Allori et al. 2013, Weinberg 2014). We will not comment further on this question here, but we observe that the choice between the two Churches is closely related to the interpretational questions discussed in Section 5.

2.2 Ontological Models

A large part of the field of quantum foundations is concerned with understanding the nature of the reality from which quantum mechanics arises. Since we are interested in finding mathematical ways of addressing conceptual questions, it is necessary to have an appropriate mathematical framework in which to pose

---

[7] A matrix M is said to be positive semi-definite if for any vector v with n entries, $v^* \times M \times v$ is positive or zero. (v^* here denotes the conjugate transpose of v.)

our questions, and the framework which is most commonly used for this purpose is the *ontological models approach*. In its modern form, this approach was first put forward and developed by Rob Spekkens, but the motivating ideas for the formalism had been floating around in the field for some time previously, and thus for the sake of continuity we will prove Bell's theorem (see Section 3) using the ontological models framework, although Bell's result predates Spekkens' work and was originally proved using slightly different language. The Spekkens contextuality theorem in Section 4 and the PBR theorem in Section 5 will also be expressed using ontological models, since they were originally parsed in that framework.

The core of the ontological models approach is very simple: we suppose that any quantum system has a real underlying state, known as its 'ontic state'. The ontic state is determined by how the system was prepared and by any subsequent transformations which have been applied to it, and when measurements are made on the system, the results of those measurements can depend only on its ontic state. It is important to reinforce that the ontic state is not assumed to have anything to do with the quantum state – it might contain all the same information as the quantum state, or less information, or more information. And of course the ontological models approach is sufficiently general that we may attempt to make ontological models of theories which are not at all like quantum mechanics and which may not even have a concept of 'state'.

Mathematically, these ideas are represented as follows. For a given system, we suppose that there exists a space Λ of possible ontic states λ. To each preparation procedure P which can be performed on the system, we assign a probability distribution p_P over ontic states, such that $p_P(\lambda)$ gives the probability that the system will end up in the ontic state λ when we perform procedure P; to each transformation T which can be applied to the system, we assign a column-stochastic matrix T[8] describing how the distribution over ontic states is affected by this transformation; and to each measurement M which can be performed on the system and every possible outcome O of that measurement, we assign a response function $\xi_{M,O}$ such that $\xi_{M,O}(\lambda)$ gives the probability that outcome O will occur when we perform measurement M on a system which is in ontic state λ.

Suppose now that we aim for our ontological model to be capable of reproducing the empirical results of quantum theory. This imposes a number of constraints on the space of ontic states Λ, distributions p_P, transformations T and response functions $\xi_{M,O}$. For example, suppose we perform a preparation

---

[8] A column-stochastic matrix is a matrix containing only non-negative real values such that the columns of the matrix all sum to 1.

procedure P which, according to quantum mechanics, prepares the quantum state $|\psi\rangle$, and then we perform a measurement M with outcomes M_1, M_2 which, according to quantum mechanics, is represented by the POVM $\{O_1, O_2\}$: quantum mechanics tells us that the probability of obtaining outcome M_1 is equal to $Tr(O_1|\psi\rangle\langle\psi|)$. In order for our ontological model to reproduce this result, it must be the case that the probability of obtaining a given ontic state λ times the probability of obtaining outcome M_1 to measurement M when the system is in state λ, summed over all λ, gives $Tr(O_1|\psi\rangle\langle\psi|)$. That is:

$$\sum_\lambda p_P(\lambda)\xi_{M,M_1}(\lambda) = Tr(O_1|\psi\rangle\langle\psi|)$$

And if the set of ontic states is infinite, the sum becomes an integral:

$$\int p_P(\lambda)\xi_{M,M_1}(\lambda) = Tr(O_1|\psi\rangle\langle\psi|)$$

It is clear that imposing this requirement for all possible quantum mechanical preparations and measurements places very strong limitations on an ontological model, and much of the progress in quantum foundations over the last 50 years has essentially been concerned with following up the consequences of these limitations and attempting to understand what properties an ontological model must have if it is to faithfully reproduce quantum mechanics. The idea is that this will give us leading a better understanding of what the reality underlying quantum mechanics must look like in order to produce the empirical results that we have observed.

An important question about the ontological models approach concerns what exactly an ontic state should be ascribed to. We have said that every system is to be assigned an ontic state, but what is a 'system' in this context? For example, if we perform a joint preparation on two quantum systems and then separate them, should we assign separate ontic states to each of the particles, or a single joint state to both? We will see in Section 3 that there are good reasons to use a single joint state in at least some such cases, but this is not obvious before we start on the work of analysing quantum mechanics. Clearly, then, the ontological models approach has a certain vagueness, but this is actually a feature, not a bug: the whole idea is to have a framework general enough to encompass many different hypotheses about what the reality underlying quantum mechanics might look like, and in order to achieve this it is important not to be too prescriptive.

It should also be reinforced that one can make use of the formalism of ontological models without necessarily interpreting it as an attempt at a faithful representation of reality – indeed, Spekkens himself prefers to regard it as a classification schema which enables us to give precise mathematical definitions for concepts like contextuality (Spekkens, n.d.) (see Section 4). Nonetheless, it seems to be the case that within quantum foundations this formalism or something close to it is often regarded as a description of reality and perhaps as the only possible way of describing reality – for example, in Leifer and Pusey (2017), it is claimed that any model in which correlations are not explained by appeal to ontic states should not really be regarded as a realist model at all. Indeed we shall see that the view of reality enshrined in the ontological models formulation is so ubiquitous in quantum foundations that most of the important results of the field make sense only in that context.

2.3 Quantum Field Theory

Because particles in scattering experiments are frequently accelerated almost to the speed of light, it is not possible to neglect relativistic effects in the description of scattering experiments, and therefore in order to do particle physics accurately, it is necessary to make some adjustments to standard quantum mechanics. There exists a relativistic formulation of quantum mechanics where the Schrödinger equation is replaced by the Klein-Gordon and Dirac equations, but it turns out that this is not sufficient to allow us to study particle physics, because both non-relativistic and relativistic quantum mechanics are defined only for scenarios that can be described by a finite, constant number of degrees of freedom, whereas in particle physics it is necessary to describe fields with an infinite number of degrees of freedom and scattering processes in which particles may be created or destroyed. Thus, in order to apply quantum mechanics to this realm, it has been necessary to create an extension of the theory accommodating an infinite number of degrees of freedom. This extension, which has become known as quantum field theory, allows us to model successfully almost all features of elementary particle physics – gravity alone, among the fundamental forces, still resists being cast in this form (Peskin and Schroeder 1995, Lancaster and Blundell 2014).

One might ask at this juncture why anyone should persist in studying the foundations of quantum mechanics when quantum mechanics has already been supplanted by a more advanced theory. A first answer is that quantum field theory is essentially the result of applying quantum mechanics to a new domain and following up the varied and sometimes unexpected consequences, so the underlying principles of quantum field theory are very close to the underlying principles of quantum mechanics and one might expect that most of the interesting conceptual issues that arise in quantum field theory will already appear in quantum mechanics. Moreover, quantum field theory has many mathematical complexities that do not exist in standard quantum mechanics and actually is not yet a consistent and complete theory, which makes foundational questions much more difficult to answer and even to pose (Kuhlmann 2018). That said, it is important to be aware of the relativistic theory and to keep in mind that any conclusions we might draw from the study of quantum foundations must ultimately be understood in a relativistic context. In the course of this Element we will see that some of the cornerstones of the field may indeed have a quite different significance when considered in this light.

3 Bell's Theorem and Non-locality

3.1 Bell's Theorem

Consider the following experimental procedure:

1. Two quantum systems are prepared together, then one system is sent to experimenter A and the second system is sent to experimenter B, the two experimenters being located at some spatial separation.
2. At a pre-arranged time, experimenter A chooses one of two possible measurements M_1^A and M_2^A and performs this measurement on their system. M_1^A and M_2^A each have two possible outcomes, which will be labelled by 1 and -1.
3. Likewise, experimenter B chooses one of two possible measurements M_1^B and M_2^B and performs this measurement on their system. M_1^B and M_2^B each have two possible outcomes, which will be labelled by 1 and -1.

Using the ontological models framework, we suppose that the original joint preparation gives rise to an ontic state λ from some set of ontic states $\{\lambda\}$, with preparation probabilities $p(\lambda)$. For any pair of measurements $(M_i^A, M_j^B) : i, j \in \{0, 1\}$, we can define response functions $p(s, t | \lambda, M^A = i, M^B = j)$, which give the probability of obtaining the two results s, t when measurements (M_i^A, M_j^B) are performed and the joint ontic state is λ. We may also define response functions on the individual systems, so for example the response function $p^A(s | \lambda, M^A = i, M^B = j, O^B = t)$ gives the probability that experimenter A obtains outcome s when measurements (M_i^A, M_j^B) are performed and the joint ontic state is λ and experimenter B obtains outcome t. (We condition on B obtaining outcome t in case it is possible to for B's result to alter the post-measurement joint ontic state λ.)

Let us now suppose that any correlation between the results obtained by experimenters A and B is local – that is, that the result of the measurement made by experimenter A must depend only on their own choice of measurement and the original joint ontic state λ, so the response functions $p^A(s|\lambda, M^A = i, M^B = j, O^B = t)$ can be written as $p^A(s|\lambda, M^A = i)$ with no dependence on B's choice of measurement or outcome; likewise for the response functions for experimenter B. The ontological model is therefore *factorisable* as follows:

$$p(s, t|\lambda, M^A = i, M^B = j) = p^A(s|\lambda, M^A = i)p^B(t|\lambda, M^B = j)$$

Let $E_\lambda(i,j)$ be the expectation value of the product of the two measurement results when the measurements (M_i^A, M_j^B) are performed and the joint ontic state is λ. Then let $E(i,j)$ be the average of this expectation value over all the ontic states, weighted by the preparation probabilities, i.e. $E(i,j) = \int_\lambda p(\lambda)E_\lambda(i,j)$. We can then define what is known as the CHSH quantity:

$$S = |E(0,0) + E(0,1) + E(1,0) - E(1,1)|$$

Let $S_\lambda = |E_\lambda(0,0) + E_\lambda(0,1) + E_\lambda(1,0) - E_\lambda(1,1)|$ be the value of S conditional on some particular joint ontic state λ. Then, since the absolute value of the average of a quantity cannot be greater than the average of its absolute value, we have

$$S \leq \int_\lambda p(\lambda)S_\lambda$$

The factorisability condition implies that the expectation values for the two measurements likewise factorise; if $A_\lambda(i)$ is the expectation value of experimenter A's outcome when they perform measurement M_i^A and the joint ontic state is λ, and likewise for $B_\lambda(j)$, then

$$E_\lambda(i,j) = A_\lambda(i)B_\lambda(j)$$

Thus, for any λ,

$$S_\lambda = |A_\lambda(0)B_\lambda(0) + A_\lambda(0)B_\lambda(1) + A_\lambda(1)B_\lambda(0) - A_\lambda(1)B_\lambda(1)|$$

$$\leq |A_\lambda(0)B_\lambda(0) + A_\lambda(0)B_\lambda(1)| + |A_\lambda(1)B_\lambda(0) - A_\lambda(1)B_\lambda(1)|$$

$$= |A_\lambda(0)||B_\lambda(0) + B_\lambda(1)| + |A_\lambda(1)||B_\lambda(0) - B_\lambda(1)|$$

$$\leq |B_\lambda(0) + B_\lambda(1)| + |B_\lambda(0) - B_\lambda(1)|$$

where at the second line we have used the triangle inequality, i.e. the fact that for any real or imaginary numbers a and b it is always the case that $|a + b| \leq |a| + |b|$, and at the last line we have used the fact that the measurement outcomes are labelled by -1 and 1 and thus the expectation values $A_\lambda(i), B_\lambda(i)$ must all lie between -1 and 1, so $|A_\lambda(0)| \leq 1$.

Now observe that $|B_\lambda(0) + B_\lambda(1)| + |B_\lambda(0) - B_\lambda(1)|$ equals two times the maximum of $|B_\lambda(0)|$ and $|B_\lambda(1)|$ (if you are not convinced, try a few examples), and since both these expectation values must likewise be less than or equal to one, we have that

$$S_\lambda \leq 2$$

Since this holds for any λ, it must also hold for the average over λ and hence

$$S \leq 2$$

3.2 Non-locality

It is a basic fact of our experience that our actions affect only those objects which are spatially co-located with us at the time of the action, and that we can influence more distant objects only by means of some mediating physical process – so, for example, we cannot communicate ideas instantaneously to people on the other side of the world, and are instead forced to take recourse to some mediating physical process such as putting a letter in the post. Further examination of the macroscopic world seems to bear out the conjecture that this constraint applies quite generally across the classical world, and therefore in classical physics it was more or less taken for granted that there could be no action at a distance.[9]

But in the world of quantum mechanics, it seems this simple observation might no longer hold. Look back at the fourth postulate of quantum mechanics in Section 2.1 – it tells us that if we prepare the parts of a composite system independently and then combine them, the resulting joint state will be a tensor product of states on the individual parts of the system. But it is possible to produce other types of joint states, for example by applying a unitary operation

---

[9] Though there exist a few interesting exceptions – see Hesse (1955).

to two systems at once, or performing a measurement on both of them together, and in some cases the result of such a procedure will be an *entangled* state, i.e. a state which can no longer be written as the tensor product of states on the individual subsystems. Such composite systems have global properties that cannot be reduced to separate properties of the individual subsystems (Wiseman 2006, Maudlin 2011, Nielsen and Chuang 2011), which was not a state of affairs that ever arose in classical physics and which opens up the possibility of genuine action at a distance.

It might be tempting to suppose that entanglement is no more than a quirk of our choice of mathematical representation, but in 1964 John Bell showed that its existence has profound physical consequences (Bell 1964, Bell 1966, Shimony 2013). To do so, Bell studied 'local hidden variable models' – that is, models in which all correlations between measurements on different systems can be traced back to correlations between hidden variables of the systems that were established during a local interaction at some point in their common past. Bell's theorem, which we prove in Box 3.1, states that in any such model, given two systems and two different measurements $\{M_1^A, M_2^A\}$, and $\{M_1^B, M_2^B\}$ for each of the two systems respectively, each of these four measurements having two possible outcomes labelled by $+1$ or -1, if $E(i, j)$ denotes the expectation value of the product of the two measurement results when we perform M_i^A and M_j^B on the two systems respectively, then the following inequality, known as the CHSH inequality,[10] must be satisfied:

$$|E(0, 0) + E(0, 1) + E(1, 0) - E(1, 1)| \leq 2 \qquad (3.1)$$

But there exist entangled quantum systems exhibiting correlations that violate this inequality, and therefore quantum mechanics cannot be fully explained by any local hidden variable model (Clauser et al. 1969). Moreover, the existence of these correlations has been verified by rigorous experiments successively eliminating larger and larger numbers of possible loopholes (Aspect et al. 1981, Kielpinski et al. 2001, Hensen et al. 2015), so it seems that unless we wish to eschew a realist description of nature altogether, we are forced to postulate some kind of 'spooky action at a distance' (Einstein et al. 1935) to explain the correlations.

To appreciate the significance of this result, it is important to distinguish the quantum correlations from more familiar sorts of distant correlations. In his

---

[10] Bell originally proved a related but different inequality, but the CHSH inequality originally proved by Clauser, Horne, Shimony, and Holt (Clauser et al. 1969) is more commonly used in modern quantum foundations research, and hence we employ it here and throughout this Element.

essay 'Bertlmann's Socks and the Nature of Reality' (Bell 1987), Bell explains this by analogy to socks. Suppose I take a pair of socks from a drawer, separate them without looking at them, and then send one sock to Japan and another to Brazil. My colleagues in Japan and Brazil open their packages at the same time and immediately report their results to me: lo and behold, both socks are red! Of course, there is nothing mysterious about this distant, instantaneous correlation – it occurs because the socks were paired up before being separated, i.e. it can be accounted for in terms of local interactions in the past. But Bell's theorem shows that there exist correlations in quantum mechanics which *cannot* be explained in this way: no matter how much information is shared between the two quantum systems in the Bell experiment at the time when they are together, it is not possible to achieve the kind of coordinated measurement results exhibited by quantum mechanics using only that shared information. The mathematics seems to be telling us that the choice of measurement on one particle must instantaneously influence the state of the other particle, even if the measurements are made almost simultaneously at very distant locations.

3.3 Relativity

The emergence of Bell's theorem caused a great deal of consternation within the physics community, and not only because it does violence to our everyday intuitions. For Bell's theorem also puts quantum mechanics in tension, if not outright contradiction, with another very important and well-established area of physics – Einstein's theories of Special and General Relativity (Einstein 1920, Sartori 1996).

Special and General Relativity were developed around the same time as quantum mechanics, but they cover an entirely different domain: while quantum mechanical effects largely occur at the microscopic scale, Special and General Relativity are theories of space and time and are most easily observed in very large-scale experiments. Both theories have a wide array of interesting and varied consequences, but for our present purposes, two are particularly important. First, relativity tells us that it is impossible to send a signal faster than light (the 'no-signalling principle'), and second, relativity tells us that there is no such thing as absolute simultaneity. That is, given two spatially separated points a, b, then if some event A takes place at a, there is no fact of the matter about what is happening at b at the same time as A. Observers in different 'reference frames', i.e. moving at different speeds relative to one another, will come to different conclusions about which event at b is simultaneous with A, and none of them will have any better claim to validity than any of the others. Indeed, if we place a clock C_b at b, then for any time t as measured by C_b such that a beam of light produced at b when clock C_b read t could not have reached a before event A, and also a beam of light produced at a at the same time as event A could not have reached b by the time that C_b reads t, then there exists some frame of reference in which C_b reads t at the same time as event A.

This is problematic for quantum mechanics, because it means that in a relativistic context it makes no sense to say that a measurement on one particle instantaneously influences the state of some other spatially separated particle, since there is no objectively correct way to say which times are 'instantaneous' for the two distant locations. Indeed, for certain configurations of distant measurements, we can change the temporal ordering between the two measurements by simply changing reference frames, so there cannot even be a well-defined causal account of the sequence of events: in one reference frame, the measurement on particle A instantaneously changes the state of particle B, and in another reference frame the measurement on particle B instantaneously changes the state of particle A. So these instantaneous influences are not even well-defined in a relativistic context, and yet Bell's theorem seems to tell us that they must occur in nature.

Of course, contradictions between theories are not necessarily regarded as an evil by physicists: contradictions provide opportunities for empirical tests that distinguish between the two theories, and that means progress. But in a further infuriating twist, it turns out that quantum mechanics also obeys a constraint known as the no-signalling theorem, which tells us that performing transformations or measurements on one part of an entangled system never changes the state of the other part in a way that can be used for information transfer (Walleczek and Grössing 2014). Now, the quantum-mechanical and special relativistic no-signalling constraints are not identical, and neither one implies the other: the relativistic no-signalling principle does not rule out information transfer via measurements on entangled systems in cases where one measurement is sufficiently close in time and space to the other, while the quantum-mechanical no-signalling theorem has nothing to say about whether an object can physically travel faster than light. Nonetheless, in practical terms the fact that quantum mechanics is non-signalling ensures that it does not make any empirical predictions that contradict relativity, which means we cannot use the incompatibility between the theories to design an experiment which will simply tell us that one is right and the other is wrong. Instead, we are faced with a more difficult situation where both theories work perfectly in their own domains, yet we have no coherent story about the sort of universe in which they could both by true.

One possible response to this situation is to adopt a form of anti-realism – either as an explicit philosophical position, or implicitly by taking the 'shut up and calculate' approach favoured by some physicists. Proponents of this approach say that as long as there is no empirical contradiction between the theories, it is not the task of physics to understand what sort of underlying reality could be compatible with them both. This, of course, is unlikely to be satisfactory to anyone who has come to quantum foundations out of an interest in understanding how the world really is, but it is short-sighed even for people who take a purely empiricist point of view, because one of the major outstanding problems of physics is to find a theory which unifies quantum mechanics and general relativity, and addressing what seems to be an irresolvable conflict between their underlying principles is likely to be a good way to make progress on this point (Hardy and Spekkens 2010).

3.3.1 Superdeterminism

One way of resolving this conflict is to insist that Bell's theorem does not after all imply that the world is non-local. After all, the violation of the CHSH inequality by quantum mechanics proves only that *one* of the assumptions that goes into the derivation of the inequality must be wrong, so perhaps we can keep locality and reject some other assumption instead. A promising candidate is the assumption known as 'statistical independence' – that is, the assumption that the value of the hidden variable λ describing the joint state of the composite system is independent of the choices made by the experimenters about which measurements to perform (Horne et al. 1993, Hossenfelder and Palmer 2020).

At first, the idea of statistical independence being violated seems very startling, since in physics we normally assume that experimenters are external to the system being experimented on and can make free choices about which experiments to perform. But it should be kept in mind that the freedom of choice that we attribute to experimenters was only ever an idealisation: in real life, experimenters are physically embodied and their choices have physical causes which could in principle be correlated with the systems they are measuring.[11] Thus it is perfectly coherent to suppose that the experimenters' choices and the hidden variable λ could in fact have some joint physical cause which lies in their common past (or perhaps in their common future – see Section 3.3.3).

Nonetheless, one might worry that violations of statistical independence would threaten the possibility of doing science at all, since statistical independence plays a crucial role in much of our ordinary scientific reasoning

---

[11] Of course anyone who espouses mind-body dualism (Robinson 2017) will not agree with this, and thus mind-body dualists may be less likely than others to find the rejection of statistical independence compelling, but mind-body dualism does not seem to be a particularly popular view among modern physicists.

(Clauser et al. 1969). For example, consider a scenario where we can choose to perform a measurement determining whether a system has property A, or to perform a measurement determining whether a system has property B, but we cannot perform both measurements on the same system. Say we perform the same preparation procedure P 100,000 times, then check for property A on half of the resulting system, and check for property B on the remaining half. If all 50,000 of our A-measurements yield a negative result, we would be inclined to conclude that procedure P never produces a system with property A. However, if statistical independence does not hold, it could be the case that there's some 'joint physical cause' which arranges that whenever we measure A the system does not have property A, but whenever we measure B, the system *does* have property A. Thus the violation of statistical independence allows for all sorts of conspiratorial behaviour which would seem to undermine the possibility of scientific knowledge.

However, it should be kept in mind that this is not the first time we have been confronted with putative features of the world which seemed to threaten the integrity of the scientific method – for example, Einstein famously objected to the possibility of non-locality on the grounds that if we accepted this suggestion, 'physical thinking in the familiar sense would not be possible' (Einstein 1948). Yet it has not proven to be impossible to formulate meaningful physical theories which include spatial non-locality, because the non-local relations between events are governed by laws which enable us to identify regularities in patterns of dependence even between spatially separated events. Likewise, in principle it would not be impossible to move forward with a theory which allows for violations of statistical independence, provided that the resulting relationships still exhibit regularities of the right kind.

The rejection of statistical independence is particularly associated with 'superdeterminism' (Bell 1985, Hossenfelder and Palmer 2020), referring to hidden variables theories which are local and deterministic and which get around Bell's theorem by violating statistical independence. A deterministic theory is one in which all outcomes of a measurement can be predicted with certainty, provided that we have sufficiently precise information about the initial conditions; classical physics is deterministic,[12] but quantum physics in its standard form is not, and some proponents of hidden-variable theories have hoped to use hidden variables as a way of bringing determinism back. The association between locality and determinism is partly historical: in Bell's original work, he showed that any theory which is both local *and* deterministic must obey a certain inequality which is violated by quantum mechanics (Bell 1966),

---

[12] Apart from in very special cases (Hoefer 2016).

so violating statistical independence was then seen as a way to rescue the possibility of local deterministic hidden variable theories. But later versions of Bell's theorem, such as the version we proved in Box 3.1, showed that *any* local theory, whether deterministic or not, must obey an inequality which is violated by quantum mechanics, and this means that strictly speaking it is locality and not determinism that needs rescuing by the rejection of statistical independence (Clauser et al. 1969, Buttereld 1992).

Nonetheless, there is logic to the continued association between determinism and locality, because special and general relativity are local[13] deterministic theories, and it seems almost as hard to see how a deterministic theory could be unified with an indeterministic one as to see how a local theory could be unified with a non-local one (Seevinck 2010). By proposing that the theory underlying quantum mechanics may be both local and deterministic, superdeterminism removes both fundamental incompatibilities at once, and its proponents argue that it therefore offers new hope of reconciling quantum mechanics and relativity (Hossenfelder and Palmer 2020).

3.3.2 Temporal Non-locality

A different approach to resolving the tension between quantum mechanics and relativity is to accept the existence of spatial non-locality and observe that the root of the incompatibility with relativity lies not in non-locality per se but rather in the assumption that the non-local influences must occur *instantaneously*, which makes no sense in a relativistic context. But, after all, why should the non-local influence be instantaneous? In making this demand, we are assuming that although the influence of the measurement of one particle on the state of the other may be non-local in space, it must still be local in time: we remain wedded to the notion that the past can influence the future only via information carried in mediating states that evolve forwards in time. If on the other hand we simply say that the choice of measurement on one particle *directly* influences the outcome of the measurement on the second particle, wherever and whenever that measurement occurs, then the apparent contradiction with relativity goes away. And indeed this is to be expected, because insisting on temporal locality while allowing spatial non-locality means that we are treating space and time in entirely different ways, and it is hardly surprising that

---

[13] That is, they are local in the sense that they do not allow for action-at-a-distance. Arguably there is a sense in which General Relativity is not local in the traditional sense; see Section 3.3.2 for details.

this leads to contradictions with relativity given that one of the key messages of relativity is that space and time are very closely related.[14]

Temporally non-local approaches to quantum mechanics have not been well-explored, perhaps because physicists tend to think of the universe as a kind of computer which takes as input an initial state and then evolves it forward in time in a temporally local way (Wharton 2015). However, it is straightforward to describe a few forms that such approaches might take. For example, a theory might be temporally non-local by postulating non-Markovian laws, meaning that the results of a measurement at a given time can depend on facts about earlier times, even if there is no record of those facts in the state of the world at the time of the measurement. Note that this type of temporal non-locality makes sense only if the state of the world at a given time does not give us complete information about the past – in classical physics, for example, the entire past and entire future can be inferred from the present state of the world together with the laws of evolution, so classical physics cannot exhibit this sort of temporal non-locality. Alternatively, a theory might be temporally non-local by being global, meaning that the course of history is determined "all at once" by external, atemporal laws of nature. In such a theory, the result of a measurement at a given time can depend on global facts even if there is no record of those facts in the state of the world immediately prior to the measurement, and therefore events at different times can have a direct influence on one another without any mediation. Furthermore, an event at a given time will usually depend not only on events in the past but also on events in the future, so retrocausality (see Section 3.3.3) emerges naturally within this global picture.

The second type of temporal non-locality is particularly promising for several reasons. First, we already have working examples of such theories, since even classical mechanics can be written in a 'Lagrangian' formulation in which the path taken by a system is determined by optimising a quantity called the Lagrangian over the whole path (Brizard 2008). Quantum mechanics can also be given a Lagrangian formulation in which quantum amplitudes are calculated by taking a sum over an infinity of possible trajectories (MacKenzie 2000). Thus global theories need not be regarded as novel or challenging – they have been present in physics all along, although for a variety of reasons these Lagrangian formulations have not usually been taken seriously as a possible description of reality.

Second, if our options for reconciling relativity and quantum mechanics are either to restore locality by denying statistical independence or to adopt a global approach, arguably the latter is a better match for general relativity.

---

[14] See (Adlam 2018b) for a more extended introduction to temporal non-locality.

For although general relativity does not allow any instantaneous action at a distance, it is also not really 'local' in the sense of classical physics, because a solution to the Einstein Field equations of general relativity is not a state of the world at a single time but rather an entire history of the universe. Thus the Einstein Field equations are in fact a paradigm example of a temporally non-local law of nature, which gives us reason to be optimistic about the prospects of uniting a temporally non-local version of quantum mechanics with relativity (Adlam 2018b).

3.3.3 Retrocausality

Another assumption that goes into the derivation of Bell's theorem is that there is no retrocausality – that is, measurement results depend only on facts about the past, not the future. Retrocausality first became a topic of interest in quantum foundations when it was observed that allowing backwards causality gives us a way to explain the violation of Bell's inequality without recourse to non-locality (Price 1994; Goldstein and Tumulka 2003): the correlations between the measurement results are mediated not by 'action-at-a-distance' but by information that propagates *backwards* in time from the moment *after* the measurements at which all the information about the measurements is brought back together. One might object that here we are saving one classical intuition only by virtue of sacrificing another, so it is not clear that much progress has really been made – but since spatial non-locality is one of the major reasons for the tension between quantum mechanics and relativity, introducing retrocausality might seem like a cost worth paying to get rid of it.

The case for retrocausality became stronger when Price put forward an argument that any time-symmetric ontology satisfying certain conditions must be retrocausal (Price 2010). Now one might think that really any time-symmetric theory which incorporates forward causality must also incorporate backward causality, but this does not seem to be the case in classical physics, which has completely time-symmetric laws but which we understand in terms of causality which goes only forward in time. However Price used a particular optical experiment to demonstrate that the discreteness of quantum mechanics makes it different in this regard: if the theory is time-symmetric, an experimenter who controls the angle of the polarizer in this experiment must have a certain amount of control over the state of the input photon, and therefore their choices must have a *retrocausal* influence on the state of the photon prior to its entering the polarizer.

Price's argument, however, works only if we suppose that the state of the photon before or after entering the polarizer is an element of reality that can be subject to a retrocausal influence, so it applies only to ψ-ontic interpretations of quantum mechanics (see Section 5). It also depends on the existence of wavefunction collapse or some other form of discreteness (see Section 5.2), so it does not apply to the Everett interpretation (see Section 5.5.2) or the de Broglie Bohm interpretation (see Section 5.5.3). To get around these shortcomings, the argument was later generalised by Pusey and Leifer (Leifer and Pusey 2017), who replaced the assumption that the quantum state is real with the assumption of λ-mediation, which they state as follows: 'any correlations between a preparation and a measurement made on a system should be mediated by the physical properties of the system'. This assumption allows them to use the ontological models approach in their analysis – or, rather, a generalisation of the ontological models approach, since in its original formulation the ontological models approach did not allow the possibility of retrocausality. Working within this approach, and using the assumption of no-retrocausality in much the same way as locality is used in the proof of Bell's theorem, they are able to prove that a theory which obeys λ-mediation and a specific sort of time symmetry, and which does not exhibit retrocausality, must obey a temporal analogue of the CHSH inequality. But in quantum mechanics this temporal inequality is violated, so it seems that we must accept retrocausality if we want time symmetry and λ-mediation.

Interestingly, λ-mediation is essentially what we referred to in the previous section as temporal locality, so what the Pusey-Leifer result proves is that if we insist on temporal locality and also time-symmetry, then some of the temporally local mediation that establishes temporal correlations must proceed backwards in time instead of forwards. Thus we are not immediately forced by this argument to accept that time-symmetry implies retrocausality: we might instead regard it as yet another nail in the coffin of temporal locality, since if temporal locality does not even allow us to hold onto classical intuitions about the direction of causality and/or time-symmetry, we have one less reason to continue insisting upon it.

On the other hand, as we observed in Section 3.3.2, a large class of temporally non-local theories would naturally incorporate retroausality anyway. It is helpful here to make a distinction between two types of retrocausal theories. First, we have retrocausal theories where there are two distinct 'arrows' of causality, one carrying information forward in time and the other carrying information back in time. A good illustration of this is the two-state vector formalism (Aharonov et al. 2014), which is a proposed interpretation of quantum mechanics in which we have both the usual forwards-evolving quantum state and also an additional backwards-evolving quantum state, so that measurement results at a given time are determined by the interaction of the forwards and backwards-evolving states at that time. The transactional interpretation of quantum theory (Cramer 1986), where the quantum state is complemented with a conjugate state which evolves backwards in time and interacts with the ordinary state in a 'Wheeler-Feynman handshake', is also a theory of this type. This is also the kind of retrocausality that is invoked in popular accounts of time travel, leading to what is known as the 'grandfather paradox', i.e. the objection that if backwards time travel were possible a time traveller could go back in time and kill their own grandfather. Of course, positing the existence of retrocausality is not at all the same as suggesting the possibility of time travel, but nonetheless conceptual problems of the same genre do arise for this type of retrocausality – for if we have to accomodate causal arrows from both the past and the future, then in order to avoid paradoxes of the grandfather type, it is important to impose strong constraints on the initial and final conditions of the universe and on the types of interactions which can occur in between (Black 1956), and this sort of fine-tuning is generally looked upon with suspicion by physicists.

But there is a second type of retrocausality – the type discussed in Section 3.3.2 which emerges from global theories postulating laws which apply to the whole of spacetime all at once. In such a theory, events at a given time are certainly in some sense 'caused' by future events, since each part of the history is dependent on all other parts of the history, but there are no distinct forwards and backwards arrows and hence no problem of ensuring agreement between past and future causes, so we do not need to worry about causal paradoxes. Furthermore, as we noted in Section 3.3.2, this sort of retrocausality is familiar to us from the Lagrangian formulations of classical and quantum physics, so we already have a good understanding of how to formulate such theories.

However, the quantum foundations community does not usually distinguish between these two types of retrocausality, which causes some confusion – many of the objections (Black 1956, Friederich and Evans 2019) that have been raised against retrocausal interpretations of quantum theory are largely

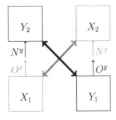

Figure 3.1 Schematic diagram of the composition of two processes

concerned with the problem of conflicting causal arrows and thus apply primarily to the first type of retrocausality, so in some cases people may be arguing at cross-purposes.

3.4 The Limits of Quantum Non-locality

Leaving aside the issue of compatibility with relativity, there are many other interesting questions to be asked about the nature of non-locality in quantum mechanics. For example, if non-local influences really exist, why are they so limited? They cannot, for example, be used to perform signalling, which makes it feel rather as if nature has deliberately conspired to hide non-locality from us.

One way of addressing this question is to observe that if it were possible to perform signalling using quantum correlations, then it would be possible to set up closed causal loops. For example, suppose Alice and Bob are in possession of two pairs of devices (X_1, X_2) and (Y_1, Y_2) such that X_1 can perform faster-than-light signalling to X_2 and Y_1 can perform faster-than-light signalling to Y_2, then consider the set-up shown in Figure 3.1: Alice reads a bit value from the output of device X_1 and then inputs it to device Y_2, so that Bob can read its value from the output of device Y_1 and then input it to device X_2, meaning that it is sent to Alice and emerges as the output of device X_1. The value of this bit has thus come out of nowhere – it has no cause outside the loop. It would be possible to avoid this conclusion by supposing that the universe has a preferred reference such that signalling is possible only in the preferred reference frame, since then signalling would be possible in only one direction between A and B so the construction of a loop would be impossible. However, it is a key postulate of the theory of special relativity that the universe has no preferred reference frame, so we have good reasons from outside quantum mechanics for rejecting this possibility. Thus if we believe that nature should not allow closed causal loops, and that the universe has no preferred reference frame, we can explain why the laws of nature should not allow signalling (Arntzenius 1994, Maudlin 2011).

On the other hand, it is not immediately obvious why nature should not allow closed causal loops to exist, provided that they do not lead to any actual contradictions (Berkovitz 2002). After all, quantum mechanics is commonly supposed to be intrinsically random, which means that the outcomes of measurements must frequently come out of nowhere, having no cause for their exact value. It may be, therefore, that to make this argument work we may need to make a stronger claim – for example, that the universe is deterministic in some generalised sense,[15] which would imply a prohibition on values coming out of nowhere in this way.

---

[15] See Adlam (2018a) for more details on this approach.

However, even if we can explain the absence of signalling by an argument of this kind, there's a further twist – for it turns out that quantum mechanics is not the most non-local theory which is compatible with no-signalling. This fact emerged via the work of Popescu and Rohrlich on non-local boxes (Rohrlich and Popescu 1995) – that is, sets of hypothetical devices which accept inputs and produce outputs which may be correlated in any mathematically describable way. Popescu and Rohrlich described a specific pair of boxes, now known as 'PR boxes', which cannot be used to perform signalling but which can be used to produce a value of 4 for the CHSH quantity defined in equation 3.1. But it has been shown by Tsirelson that no arrangement of quantum mechanical systems can produce a value greater than $2\sqrt{2}$ for the CHSH quantity (Tsirelson 1980), so the PR boxes exhibit a stronger form of non-locality than quantum mechanics.

We know, therefore, that the world is more local than it would need to be simply in order to avoid the possibility of signalling, and this has prompted a search for further constraints which might explain the limits on quantum non-locality. One interesting proposal is known as 'information causality' (Pawlowski et al. 2009). Consider the following operational task: experimenter A receives a random string of N bits, $a_0 a_2 .. a_{N-1}$, and experimenter B receives an integer value v in the interval $[0, 1, ...N-1]$. A sends B a total of m classical bits without knowing the value that B has received; B is then required to make a guess β for the value of the bit in position v of A's string. We allow that A and B may share any number of quantum resources prepared in advance of the task, though they may not exchange any quantum systems after the task begins. Information causality imposes a constraint on the probability of Bob successfully completing this task, which we express in the language of 'mutual information', a measure from classical information theory which quantifies the correlation between two variables.[16] Denote by $I(a_K : \beta | v = K)$ the mutual information between bit K in A's string and B's guess β, conditional on B receiving the value K; then information causality requires that

$$\sum_K I(a_K : \beta | v = K) \leq m$$

That is to say, information causality requires that the total amount of information that experimenter B is able to access about A's string, over all the different strategies that might be used to get information, should not be larger than the number of classical bits that A sends. Thus it is a sort of generalised

---

[16] See (Thomas and Cover 2006) for more details on classical information theory and mutual information.

no-signalling constraint on the total amount of information that agents have access to under different counterfactual conditions.

Pawlowski et al. (2009) showed that the violation of the Tsirelson bound implies that information causality is not satisfied. Thus, if we are willing to accept information causality as a fundamental constraint on physical reality, we have an explanation for the gap between the quantum and classical no-signalling bounds. Of course, opinions will vary on the idea of information causality as a fundamental physical constraint: the principle may have a plausible air, but it certainly is not logically impossible that the world should have failed to obey information causality, and so one might argue that the putative explanation is incomplete without some proposal for an underlying ontology which explains why information causality must necessarily be satisfied in the actual world.

We also know that information causality cannot be the complete explanation, because although it lets us derive the correct bound in this particular case, it does not suffice to derive the full set of quantum correlations. In particular, it is known that there exists a set of 'almost quantum correlations' which is bigger than the set of quantum correlations, but which satisfies information causality (as well as various other principles that have been proposed to explain this gap) (Navascués et al. 2015). So although principles like information causality offer tantalising hints, as yet we have no complete answer to the question of why the non-locality of quantum mechanics is limited in the specific way that it is.

4 The Kochen-Specker Theorem and Contextuality

4.1 The Kochen-Specker Theorem

We will show that there exists a set of measurements on a four-dimensional quantum system which is not consistent with deterministic non-contextuality.

Although quantum systems are defined on complex Hilbert spaces, it is sufficient for us to exhibit a set of operators on a *real* Hilbert space, since a real Hilbert space can always be mapped to a complex Hilbert space. Thus we will work with a real four-dimensional Hilbert space, where each vector represents an operator.

Each set of four orthogonal vectors in this real Hilbert space sums to the identity and thus defines a possible measurement (recall from Section 2.1 that a measurement is defined as a set of positive operators that sum to the identity). Let us try to find an assignment of the values 0, 1 to the vectors in this space which is consistent with deterministic contextuality.

Consider the following table:

(0,0,0,1)	(0,0,1,0)	(1,1,0,0)	(1,-1,0,0)
(0,0,0,1)	(0,1,0,0)	(1,0,1,0)	(1,0,-1,0)
(1,-1,1,-1)	(1,-1,-1,1)	(1,1,0,0)	(0,0,1,1)
(1,-1,1,-1)	(1,1,1,1)	(1,0,-1,0)	(0,1,0,-1)
(0,0,1,0)	(0,1,0,0)	(1,0,0,1)	(1,0,0,-1)
(1,-1,-1,1)	(1,1,1,1)	(1,0,0,-1)	(0,1,-1,0)
(1,1,-1,1)	(1,1,1,-1)	(1,-1,0,0)	(0,0,1,1)
(1,1,-1,1)	(-1,1,1,1)	(1,0,1,0)	(0,1,0,-1)
(1,1,1,-1)	(-1,1,1,1)	(1,0,0,1)	(0,1,-1,0)

There are 36 entries in this table, taken from a set of 18 vectors with every vector appearing exactly twice. In each row, we have a set of 4 orthogonal vectors, so determinism implies that our value assignment must give the value 1 to exactly one entry in each row, i.e. 9 entries in total.

But contextuality implies that each vector must be assigned the same value wherever it appears in the table, and therefore the number of entries assigned the value 1 must be equal to two times the number of vectors assigned the value 1, which cannot be an odd number.

We have found a contradiction, and therefore no value assignment for this set of vectors can obey both determinism and contextuality. This demonstrates that deterministic contextuality cannot hold universally for quantum mechanics.

4.2 Deterministic Contextuality

What exactly do we learn when we perform a measurement on a system? In classical physics, the answer seems relatively straightforward: we learn about the properties of the system. For example, when we perform a measurement to determine the charge of a particle we take it for granted that the particle has one of the properties 'positive charge', 'negative charge', or 'neutral charge', and that it cannot have more than one of these properties, so measuring its charge is a simple matter of finding out which property it has.

But it turns out that this simple view of measurement is no longer tenable in the quantum world. Recall from section 2.1.2 that a quantum measurement is represented by a POVM, i.e. a set of positive semi-definite operators which sum to the identity. This has the immediate consequence that for quantum systems of dimension greater than two, an operator may appear in more than one measurement. We give an example below of two measurements for a quantum system of dimension three which both contain the measurement operator A:[17]

Measurement 1:

$$\{A = |0\rangle\langle 0|,$$

$$B = |1\rangle\langle 1|,$$

$$C = |2\rangle\langle 2|\}$$

Measurement 2:

$$\{A = |0\rangle\langle 0|,$$

$$D = \frac{1}{2}(|1\rangle + |2\rangle)(\langle 1| + \langle 2|),$$

$$E = \frac{1}{2}(|1\rangle - |2\rangle)(\langle 1| - \langle 2|)\}$$

Now if measurement results in quantum mechanics correspond to pre-existing properties of systems, as they are assumed to do in classical physics, then for any measurement on a given quantum system, there must be exactly one operator in that measurement which corresponds to a property that the system definitely has, such that we will be certain to obtain the corresponding measurement outcome if we perform this measurement; likewise all the other operators must correspond to properties that the system definitely does not have, such that we will definitely not obtain the corresponding measurement

---

[17] By convention, the kets $|0\rangle, |1\rangle, |2\rangle$ correspond to three orthogonal vectors, e.g. $\begin{bmatrix} 1 \\ 0 \\ 0 \end{bmatrix}, \begin{bmatrix} 0 \\ 1 \\ 0 \end{bmatrix}, \begin{bmatrix} 0 \\ 0 \\ 1 \end{bmatrix}$. Using this representation, it is straightforward to see that for each of these two measurements, the three operators given are positive semi-definite and sum to the identity matrix $\begin{bmatrix} 1 & 0 & 0 \\ 0 & 1 & 0 \\ 0 & 0 & 1 \end{bmatrix}$, so they satisfy the conditions for valid POVMs.

outcomes if we perform this measurement. Moreover, if a given operator corresponds to a property which the system definitely has, then we must also obtain the corresponding measurement result if we perform any *other* measurement which includes that operator. Mathematically, we can express this condition by saying that for any given set of measurements on a quantum system it must be possible to assign the values 1 and 0 to all the operators included in this set, such that each measurement includes exactly one operator with value 1. This requirement is commonly known as 'non-contextuality', and a theory which fails to obey it is said to exhibit 'contextuality.' (Held 2014). However, we will henceforth use the term 'deterministic (non)-contextuality' for this concept, in order to distinguish it from a related form of contextuality discussed in Section 4.3.

The Kochen-Specker theorem (Kochen and Specker 1975) says that there exist sets of measurements on quantum systems of dimension greater than two such that the assignment of values 0 and 1 required for deterministic non-contextuality cannot be achieved. Kochen and Specker originally proved this using a set of 117 operators on a three-dimensional quantum system, but simpler proofs have subsequently been put forward, and in Box 4.1 we have given a proof using only 18 vectors due to Cabello, Estebaranz, and Garcia-Alcaine (Cabello et al. 1996). As a result of this theorem, we know that quantum mechanics does not in general obey deterministic contextuality, and this has forced physicists to rethink the relationship between quantum measurement outcomes and underlying features of reality. Whatever it is that measurement outcomes tell us about the world, they do not always tell us about properties that systems definitely have, at least not for quantum systems of dimensions greater than two.

To understand more precisely the way in which quantum mechanics fails to conform to our classical intuitions, it is helpful to note that deterministic contextuality can be decomposed into two parts. First, there is the idea that measurement outcomes represent stable underlying facts about systems, and second, there is the idea that measurement outcomes are deterministic – that is, given perfect knowledge of the underlying state of the system, we should be able to predict with certainty the outcome of any measurement on it. In mathematical terms, the first idea leads to the requirement that an operator must be assigned the *same* value everywhere it appears, while the second idea leads to the requirement that we should assign only values 0 and 1.

Yet quantum mechanics itself is not a deterministic theory, and although the question of how the probabilities produced by quantum mechanics should be interpreted remains a vexed question (see Section 5), one influential view is that these probabilities reflect fundamental indeterminacies in nature. If this is indeed the case, then it will be fruitless to look for deterministic models of quantum theory – rather we should be allowing the values assigned to operators to range between 0 and 1, reflecting the probabilities of obtaining the corresponding outcome when we perform a measurement containing that operator. This suggests that there may be a way out of the Kochen-Specker theorem: we could reject the requirement of determinism but retain the idea that measurement outcomes represent the same underlying properties no matter which measurement they appear in.

4.3 Spekkens Contextuality

4.3.1 The Spekkens Contextuality Theorem

We will work within the ontological models paradigm, employing an ontological model to represent quantum mechanics. We make two additional stipulations about the model:

1. Consider two preparation procedures P and Q such that there exists a measurement distinguishing between these preparations with certainty; then the associated probability distributions $\mu_P(\lambda)$ and $\mu_Q(\lambda)$ must be non-overlapping, i.e. there is no ontic state to which they both assign a non-zero probability.

   (This follows from the requirement that an ontological model for quantum mechanics should be able to reproduce all the empirical predictions of the theory – since if there were some ontic state λ to which both distributions assigned a non-zero probability, then when we performed one of these preparations and got state λ the distinguishing measurement would sometimes give the 'wrong' result, in contradiction with the stipulation that it distinguishes the two preparations with certainty.)

2. For two preparations P and Q, consider a composite preparation procedure where we perform preparation P with probability p and preparation Q with probability $1-p$. The resulting distribution over ontic states is given by $p\mu_P(\lambda) + (1-p)\mu_Q(\lambda)$ and likewise for more complex convex sums.

   (Here we are simply assuming that probabilities over ontic states compose with other probabilities in the usual way – so, for example, if preparation P has probability 0.3 of preparing state λ, and preparation Q has probability 0.8 of preparing state λ, then if we flip a fair coin, then perform P if the result is heads, and Q if the result is tails, the overall probability of producing λ should be $0.5 \times 0.3 + 0.5 \times 0.8$.)

Let us now consider a set of six possible preparations which give rise to six different pure quantum states:

$$P_1 : \psi_1 = |0\rangle$$

$$P_2 : \psi_2 = |1\rangle$$

$$P_3 : \psi_3 = \frac{1}{2}|0\rangle + \frac{\sqrt{3}}{2}|1\rangle$$

$$P_4 : \psi_4 = \frac{\sqrt{3}}{2}|0\rangle - \frac{1}{2}|1\rangle$$

$$P_5 : \psi_5 = \frac{1}{2}|0\rangle - \frac{\sqrt{3}}{2}|1\rangle$$

$$P_6 : \psi_6 = \frac{\sqrt{3}}{2}|0\rangle + \frac{1}{2}|1\rangle$$

Then let $P_{i,j} : i,j \in \{1,2,3,4,5,6\}$ be the composite preparation procedure where either preparation P_i or P_j is performed with equal probability. Likewise let $P_{i,j,k} : i,j,k \in \{1,2,3,4,5,6\}$ be the composite preparation procedure where P_i, P_j or P_k is performed with equal probability.

Each of these preparation procedures gives rise to a mixed state, as described in Section 2.1.2; and in fact, the six states have been selected such that all of the preparations $P_{1,2}$, $P_{3,4}$, $P_{5,6}$, $P_{1,3,5}$, and $P_{2,4,6}$, give rise to the same mixed state, $\frac{1}{2}|0\rangle\langle0| + \frac{1}{2}|1\rangle\langle1|$.

Let us suppose this ontological model is preparation non-contextual. Then every way of preparing the mixed state $\frac{1}{2}|0\rangle\langle0| + \frac{1}{2}|1\rangle\langle1|$ must give rise to the same probability distribution $\mu(\lambda)$ over ontic states. Using stipulation 2, it follows that this probability distribution can be decomposed in the following different ways:

$$\mu(\lambda) = \frac{1}{2}\mu_{P_1}(\lambda) + \frac{1}{2}\mu_{P_2}(\lambda)$$

$$\mu(\lambda) = \frac{1}{2}\mu_{P_3}(\lambda) + \frac{1}{2}\mu_{P_4}(\lambda)$$

$$\mu(\lambda) = \frac{1}{2}\mu_{P_5}(\lambda) + \frac{1}{2}\mu_{P_6}(\lambda)$$

$$\mu(\lambda) = \frac{1}{3}\mu_{P_1}(\lambda) + \frac{1}{3}\mu_{P_3}(\lambda) + \frac{1}{3}\mu_{P_5}(\lambda)$$

$$\mu(\lambda) = \frac{1}{3}\mu_{P_2}(\lambda) + \frac{1}{3}\mu_{P_4}(\lambda) + \frac{1}{3}\mu_{P_6}(\lambda)$$

Now observe that states ψ_1 and ψ_2 are orthogonal, which means there exists a measurement which distinguishes them with certainty. Thus the probability distributions μ_{p1} and μ_{p2} are non-overlapping, which means that $\mu_{p1} \cdot \mu_{p2} = 0$, where the dot denotes the inner product; likewise for the pairs $(3, 4)$ and $(5, 6)$.

Let us now consider the values of the probability distributions $\mu_{P_1}...\mu_{P_6}$ at some fixed λ. Since $\mu_{p1} \cdot \mu_{p2} = 0$, and since all the entries in these vectors are probabilities and therefore cannot be negative, either $\mu_{P_1}(\lambda)$ or $\mu_{P_2}(\lambda)$ must be zero, and likewise for $\mu_{P_3}(\lambda)$, $\mu_{P_4}(\lambda)$ and $\mu_{P_5}(\lambda)$, $\mu_{P_6}(\lambda)$. Suppose we have $\mu_{P_1}(\lambda) = \mu_{P_3}(\lambda) = \mu_{P_5}(\lambda) = 0$; then from our fourth decomposition of μ we infer that $\mu(\lambda) = 0$. Suppose we have $\mu_{P_1}(\lambda) = \mu_{P_3}(\lambda) = \mu_{P_6}(\lambda) = 0$; then by combining the third and fourth decompositions of μ, we find that $\frac{1}{2}\mu_{P_5}(\lambda) = \frac{1}{3}\mu_{P_5}(\lambda)$, which is possible only if $\mu_{P_5}(\lambda) = 0$, and therefore again we have $\mu(\lambda) = 0$. From the symmetry of the problem, it is straightforward to see that any other assignation of zeroes will also yield $\mu(\lambda) = 0$.

Since this argument did not depend on the value of λ, it follows that $\mu(\lambda) = 0$ for any λ. But then μ is not a probability distribution at all and so it cannot represent the mixed state $\frac{1}{2}|0\rangle\langle 0| + \frac{1}{2}|1\rangle\langle 1|$. We have derived a contradiction; it follows that quantum mechanics cannot be represented by a preparation non-contextual ontological model.

To investigate the possibility of non-deterministic non-contextuality, let us consider a generalised notion of contextuality developed by Spekkens Spekkens (2005). The idea behind Spekkens's approach is that when we try to understand what quantum mechanics says about the world, it is natural to

suppose that any situations which are operationally equivalent should correspond to the same underlying reality, and thus should be represented identically
in an ontological model. Here, two situations are understood to be operationally
equivalent if they always lead to the same experimental statistics – so, for
example, two preparation procedures are operationally equivalent iff for any
measurement procedure we might perform after the preparation, either preparation procedure will yield the same outcome probabilities. This is essentially a
form of Occam's razor – all else being equal, we should avoid introducing com-
plications into our ontological hypotheses that do not appear in the operational
statistics we are trying to explain.

In particular, suppose a measurement outcome O_i appears in two different measurements $M_1 = \{O_g, O_h, O_i\}$ and $M_2 = \{O_i, O_j, O_k\}$. We can write
down an ontological model in which O_i is associated with the two response
functions ξ_{M_1, O_i} and ξ_{M_2, O_i} for these two measurements. Then observe that
from each of these measurements we can obtain a measurement $\{O_i, \mathbb{I} - O_i\}$
by combining outcomes j, k or g, h into a single outcome and discarding any
information about which one occurs. Clearly, the response functions associated with O_i are not changed by this post-processing, so O_i is still represented
by the same response functions ξ_{M_1, O_i} and ξ_{M_2, O_i} in the corresponding composite measurements. But these two ways of performing the measurement
$\{O_i, \mathbb{I} - O_i\}$ are operationally equivalent (that is to say, the probabilities for
O_i and $\mathbb{I} - O_i$ will always be the same no matter which of these ways we
choose to implement the measurement), and therefore if we are to associate
operationally equivalent situations with the same underlying reality, the two
ways of performing the measurement should be represented in the ontological model by the same set of response functions. It follows that we must have
$\xi_{M_1, O_i} = \xi_{M_2, O_i}$. That is to say, for a system in an ontic state λ, the probability
of obtaining the result O_i should be the same no matter whether we are per-
forming measurement M_1 or M_2. So the principle that operationally equivalent
procedures should have the same ontological representation can be understood
as the non-deterministic generalisation of the idea that each measurement outcome represents the same underlying property no matter which measurement
it occurs in.

Spekkens formalised this idea using the ontological models framework,
which enabled him to distinguish three different forms of contextuality:

1. **Preparation contextuality:** an ontological model is preparation non-
   contextual if for any set of preparation procedures which all produce the
   same quantum state, all the procedures are represented by the same probability distribution over ontic states; otherwise it is preparation contextual.

2. **Transformation contextuality:** an ontological model is transformation non-contextual if for any set of transformations which are all associated with the same quantum completely positive map, all the transformations are represented by the same column-stochastic matrix in the ontological model; otherwise it is transformation contextual.

3. **Measurement contextuality:** an ontological model is measurement non-contextual if for any set of measurement outcomes which are all associated with the same quantum positive operator, all the measurement outcomes are represented by the same response function in the ontological model; otherwise it is measurement contextual.

It is important to note that according to these definitions, contextuality is a property of an ontological model and not of the empirical theory which the ontological model is supposed to reproduce. This means we cannot simply say that quantum mechanics is or is not preparation/transformation/measurement non-contextual in this sense. However, Spekkens showed that *no* ontological model which is preparation non-contextual or transformation non-contextual can reproduce all the empirical results of quantum mechanics (the proof for the case of preparation contextuality is given in Box 4.3.1), and thus we are able to say that the reality underlying quantum mechanics must certainly be contextual in this particular sense. However, we do know that it is possible to construct a *measurement* non-contextual ontological model by taking the ontic states to be given by the pure quantum states and the response functions to be given by the usual quantum probabilities (this is the Beltrametti-Bugajski model) (Beltrametti and Bujaski 1995), so it remains possible that the reality underlying quantum mechanics is non-contextual when it comes to measurements.

4.4 Graph Theory and Contextuality

In a different direction, the recent work of Cabello, Severini, and Winter (Cabello et al. 2014) has uncovered an intriguing connection between quantum contextuality and graph theory. It is possible to represent a 'contextuality scenario', i.e. a set of measurement operators $\{M_i\}$ for a given quantum system, as an 'exclusivity graph', G, where every measurement operator is a vertex v of the graph and the edges E of the graph connect variables which may be simultaneously measured. We define a *probabilistic model* for such a graph by assigning nonnegative real numbers $p_v \in [0, 1]$ to the vertices v in such a way that for any edge E of the graph, $\sum_{v \in E} p_v \leq 1$. Models for a contextuality scenario that obey deterministic contextuality, known as non-contextual hidden variable (NCHV) models, are probabilistic models in which every value p_v is equal to 0 or 1.

Trivially, it is always possible to find a valid NCHV model for any contextuality scenario – for example, we can simply assign the value 0 to all vertices. However, the situation changes if we stipulate that the set of vertices of the graph includes every possible outcome for every measurement in the scenario, giving what we will describe as a *maximal* contextuality scenario. Since the sum of the probabilities for all possible outcomes to a measurement must always be one, a valid probabilistic model for a maximal scenario must satisfy $\forall E$ $\sum_{v \in E} p_v = 1$, and an NCHV model must assign the value 1 to *exactly* one vertex in each edge. It is not always possible to find even one model fulfilling these constraints: indeed, the Kochen-Specker theorem may be expressed in this language as the statement that there exist maximal contextuality scenarios which can be realised by quantum-mechanical measurements for which there exists no valid NCHV model.

For both maximal and sub-maximal contextuality scenarios, we can quantify the amount of contextuality exhibited by a model for the scenario by the expectation value of the witness operator $\Sigma := \sum_{i=1}^{q} p_i$, where p_i is the probability that we will obtain the outcome i if we perform some measurement for which i is a possible outcome, and we sum over all the vertices (Emerson et al. 2013). It can be shown (Cabello et al. 2014) that the expectation value of Σ for any valid NCHV model is bounded above by the independence number $\alpha(G)$ of the exclusivity graph.[18] On the other hand, in models where the vertices are assigned probabilities derived from a quantum-mechanical representation in terms of density operators and projective measurements, the witness operator is instead upper bounded by the Lovasz number $\theta(G)$ of the exclusivity graph.[19] Finally, in models which obey no constraint other than exclusivity – the requirement that the sum of the probabilities assigned to a set of measurement elements such that any two elements in the set are adjacent, and hence simultaneously measurable, is no greater than 1 – the witness operator is upper bounded by the fractional packing number $v_F(G)$ of the graph.[20] Now the

---

[18] The independence number of a weighted graph G is the largest sum of weights assigned to an independent set, i.e. a set such that no two two vertices in the set are adjacent (Bondy and Murty 1976).

[19] The Lovasz number of a graph G with weights $\{p_v\}$ is defined as $\sum_v p_v x_v$, where $\{x_v\}$ is a set of real numbers such that $\sum_v x_v \frac{(a_1 v)^2}{||a_v||^2} \leq 1$ for any orthogonal labelling $\{a^v\}$ (where a_1^v denotes the first entry in the vector a_v and $||a_v||$ denotes the magnitude of the vector a_v). An assignation of vectors to the vertices of a graph G is an orthonormal labelling iff the vectors representing vertices i and j are orthogonal whenever i and j are not adjacent in G.

[20] The fractional packing number of a q-vertex graph G with weights $\{p_v\}$ is equal to $\max \sum_{i \in \{1,2...q\}} p_i q_i$ where we maximise over all choices of nonnegative numbers q_i subject to the constraint that for any clique C of G, $\sum_{i \in C} q_i \leq 1$. A clique of a graph is a set of its vertices such that any two distinct vertices in the set are adjacent.

independence number, Lovasz number, and fractional packing number do not in general coincide: in general, we have $\alpha(G) \leq \theta(G) \leq \nu_F(G)$ and this suggests two interesting questions: first, why is quantum mechanics more contextual than any NCHV theory, and second, why is quantum mechanics not as contextual as exclusivity would allow? These questions may recall the discussion in Section 3.4, where we saw that quantum mechanics is more non-local than any theory which obeys locality but less non-local than no-signalling would allow – it is quite common in quantum foundations to come across scenarios of this kind, where quantum mechanics is non-classical but not *as* non-classical as it could be, which suggests that there may exist some further constraints on quantum mechanics that we have not yet got a handle on.

4.5 Contextuality and Quantum Computation

Another interesting application of contextuality is the suggestion that it may be responsible for the computational power of quantum mechanics (Howard et al. 2014). It has been known for some time that a computer using quantum systems rather than classical ones to perform calculations would be significantly more powerful than ordinary classical computers (at least, for certain specific types of computations, such as factoring large prime numbers and simulating quantum systems). But there exist a number of obstacles to getting quantum computing working in the real world, many resulting from the fact that that random noise tends to introduce errors in quantum computations. To overcome this, we use 'fault-tolerant' quantum computing, with logical encodings that make algorithms resistant to error – for example, we might perform the same computation in parallel many times and select as our final answer the result obtained by the largest number of computations.

There exist special sets of 'stabilizer' preparations, transformations and measurements which can be implemented transversally. An operation is said to be transversal if it always couples a subsystem of a code block to the corresponding subsystem in other code blocks. This means that an error in a given subsystem can only propagate to corresponding subsystems in other blocks, so transversal operations can easily be implemented in a simple fault-tolerant way (Eastin and Knill 2009). But, unfortunately, we cannot construct all possible quantum operations out of stabilizer operations alone, and indeed the Gottesman-Knill theorem proved that all stabilizer operations can be efficiently simulated by a classical computer (Gottesman 1998, Cuaro 2015), which means that none of the special non-classical power of quantum computing is accessible if we limit ourselves to stabilizer operations. However, it is possible to achieve full quantum computing with stabilizer operations if we also have access to a special set of non-stabilizer states, i.e. states which cannot be prepared using stabilizer operations alone. These special states are sometimes known as 'magic states.' (Bravyi and Kitaev 2005).

Note that the set of states which can be used for this purpose cannot simply be identified as the set of non-stabilizer states. There exists a set of states known as P_{SIM}, which includes all the stabilizer states but also some non-stabilizer states, such that quantum computation using stabilizer operations supplemented only with states from P_{SIM} can always be simulated efficiently by classical computers – meaning that no state in P_{SIM} can be used as a magic state (Aaronson and Gottesman 2004, Mari and Eisert 2012). The non-stabilizer states in P_{SIM} are known as 'bound magic states' since their magic properties cannot be put to use (Veitch et al. 2012).

So what makes the magic states so special? One possible answer was put forward by Howard, Wallman, Veitch, and Emerson (Howard et al. 2014), who used the graph-theoretic ideas in Section 4.4 to derive a set of contextuality inequalities that must be satisfied by any state which can be given an NCHV model for these stabilizer measurements. (As we saw in Section 4.2, contextuality of the NCHV type can be defined only for states of more than two dimensions, and therefore these inequalities are relevant only for systems of more than two dimensions.) They then showed that for all dimensions greater than two, every state which does not belong to P_{SIM} violates one of their contextuality inequalities, whereas no state in P_{SIM} violates any contextuality inequality defined using only stabilizer measurements. It follows that in greater than two dimensions, contextuality relative to the stabilizer measurements is necessary for a state to be magic.

5 The PBR Theorem and the Measurement Problem

5.1 The PBR Theorem

Consider the following experimental procedure:

1. Two quantum systems are sent to two experimenters in two separate spacetime locations.
2. Each experimenter flips a coin: if the result is heads, they prepare their system in state $|0\rangle$, and if the result is tails, they prepare their system in state $|+\rangle = \frac{1}{\sqrt{2}}(|0\rangle + |1\rangle)$. This gives four possible joint states:
   Heads, heads : $HH = |0\rangle \otimes |0\rangle$
   Heads, tails : $HT = |0\rangle \otimes |+\rangle$

Tails, heads : $TH = |+\rangle \otimes |0\rangle$
Tails, Tails : $TT = |+\rangle \otimes |+\rangle$.

3. The two systems are brought together and the four-outcome projective measurement $\{A, B, C, D\}$ is performed, where:

$$A = \frac{1}{2}(|0\rangle \otimes |1\rangle + |1\rangle \otimes |0\rangle)(\langle 0| \otimes \langle 1| + \langle 1| \otimes \langle 0|)$$

$$B = \frac{1}{2}(|0\rangle \otimes |-\rangle + |1\rangle \otimes |+\rangle)(\langle 0| \otimes \langle -| + \langle 1| \otimes \langle +|)$$

$$C = \frac{1}{2}(|+\rangle \otimes |1\rangle + |-\rangle \otimes |0\rangle)(\langle +| \otimes \langle 1| + \langle -| \otimes \langle 0|)$$

$$D = \frac{1}{2}(|+\rangle \otimes |-\rangle + |-\rangle \otimes |+\rangle)(\langle +| \otimes \langle -| + \langle -| \otimes \langle +|)$$

where $|-\rangle = \frac{1}{\sqrt{2}}(|0\rangle - |1\rangle)$, the state orthogonal to $|+\rangle$.

Now, the probability of obtaining outcome A to this measurement when the joint state is HH is given by $Tr(A(|0\rangle \otimes |0\rangle)(\langle 0| \otimes \langle 0|)) = Tr(\frac{1}{2}(|0\rangle \otimes |1\rangle + |1\rangle \otimes |0\rangle)(\langle 0|0\rangle \otimes \langle 1|0\rangle + \langle 1|0\rangle \otimes \langle 0|0\rangle)(\langle 0| \otimes \langle 0|) = 0$, since $|0\rangle$ and $|1\rangle$ are orthogonal, meaning that $\langle 0|1\rangle = 0$.

Likewise, it can be shown that there is zero probability of obtaining outcome B when the joint state is HT, there is zero probability of obtaining outcome C when the joint state is TH is zero, and there is zero probability of obtaining outcome D when the joint state is TT.

Now suppose that there is some overlap between the set of ontic states associated with quantum state $|0\rangle$ and the set of ontic states associated with quantum state $|+\rangle$. That is, there exists some ontic state λ such that there is non-zero probability for a system to end up in ontic state λ when we prepare the quantum state $|0\rangle$, and also non-zero probability for the system to end up in ontic state λ when we prepare the quantum state $|+\rangle$.

Then suppose that the above experimental procedure is performed, and both experimenters get the result heads and thus prepare the quantum state $|0\rangle$, and on this occasion both quantum systems end up in the ontic state λ. When we perform the final measurement on this system, we cannot obtain outcome A, because the joint state is HH. So the probability of obtaining the result A when the ontic state is λ, λ is zero.

Now suppose that both the experimenters get the result tails and on this occasion both quantum systems end up in the ontic state λ. By running the same argument again, we conclude that the probability of obtaining the result D when the ontic state is λ, λ is zero. Then by considering the cases where the experimenters get (heads, tails) or (tails, heads), we conclude that when the joint state is λ, λ there is also zero probability of obtaining the result B and zero probability of obtaining the result C. So there is no measurement outcome which is allowed to occur when the ontic state is λ, λ – but after all, the measurement must have some outcome, so we have obtained a contradiction.

It follows that there cannot be any overlap between the set of ontic states associated with quantum state $|0\rangle$ and the set of ontic states associated with quantum state $|+\rangle$ if we are to reproduce the empirical results of quantum mechanics.

However, we need to prove this not only for the two specific states $|0\rangle$ and $|+\rangle$ but for any possible pair of quantum states ψ_0 and ψ_1. To do this, we generalise the above procedure so that instead of randomly preparing two systems in state ψ_0 or ψ_1, we randomly and independently prepare n systems in one of these two states, giving a joint state $|\psi_{x_1}\rangle \otimes |\psi_{x_2}\rangle \otimes \ldots \otimes |\psi_{x_n}\rangle$ with $x_1, x_2 \ldots x_n \in \{0, 1\}$. Then we show that for any two states ψ_0 or ψ_1, for large enough n there exists a measurement with 2^n outcomes where each outcome has probability zero on at least one of the possible states. $|\psi_{x_1}\rangle \otimes |\psi_{x_2}\rangle \otimes \ldots \otimes |\psi_{x_n}\rangle$. It follows that there cannot be any overlap between the set of ontic states associated with ψ_0 and ψ_1.

Thus there cannot be any overlap between the set of ontic states associated with *any* distinct pair of quantum states, so the quantum state must be an 'element of reality'.

5.2 The Measurement Problem

What exactly happens when we perform a measurement? In classical physics, a measurement is a physical process like any other physical process: it is assumed that the measuring device, the system under measurement, and even the person performing the measurement could all in principle be modelled within the theory. And indeed it seems important that this should be so, for if a physical theory cannot explain how we obtain the measurement results which constitute our evidence for the theory, then it hardly seems reasonable to say that the evidence gives us reason to believe that the theory is true or even approximately true.

But in quantum mechanics, once again, the situation is more complicated. To see this, look back at postulate three in section 2.1, which is sometimes known as the 'Born rule'. In simple terms, it says that before we perform a measurement a quantum system may be in a state which is a superposition of all the possible measurement outcomes, but when the measurement is performed the state instantaneously changes to a state associated with just one of the measurement outcomes. This process is commonly known as the 'collapse of the wavefunction'. (The term 'wavefunction' means more or less the same as 'quantum state'.)

This means, first of all, that in quantum mechanics measurement cannot be regarded as simply an act of passive observation: performing a measurement will usually change the state of the system, so we must account for the effect of measurements when we consider the evolution of systems over time. But this is not so revolutionary, for even in classical physics the idea that we could measure systems without affecting them was always an idealisation – for example, to determine an object's position by looking at it we have to bounce light rays off it, and this will inevitably change the position of the system slightly, although the effect will be indiscernible unless the system is very small. However, in classical physics the ways in which our measurements affected the systems under measurement could still be modelled by the same physics as we would use to describe systems not under observation: classically, the effect of collisions with light rays on the momentum of a small particle is the same whether or not those light rays are being used by someone to observe it. But in quantum mechanics, this is not the case, because the 'collapse' process that occurs in measurement does not occur under any other circumstances. Thus it seems that in quantum mechanics, measurement cannot be understood as a physical process like any other physical process: it is a special category all of its own.

This is a highly unsatisfactory state of affairs, because the notion of 'measurement' is not a precise one. Should we say that a measurement necessarily involves a human experimenter? But this seems too anthropocentric – we surely do not want to say that the fundamental laws of nature contain special clauses just for humans. Should we say instead that measurement requires only a conscious observer? But then we will need to say something about what consciousness is and where its borders lie, which is a notoriously difficult problem. Or does wavefunction collapse result from a specific sort of physical interaction, which occurs in the processes that we refer to as measurements but may also occur in processes which do not involve any experimenter or consciousness? If that is so we ought to be able to say something about what that interaction is and ideally find ways to put the hypothesis to the test.

This difficulty is known as the 'measurement problem' and many people working in the foundations of physics believe that it represents a serious epistemological crisis for quantum mechanics (Wallace 2007): we still have no coherent story about how we actually come to obtain the measurement results which are our evidence for the theory, and in the absence of such a story we can hardly claim to have a complete theory. This crisis has prompted many attempts to solve the measurement problem by proposing some specific hypothesis about the reality underlying quantum mechanics which explains what actually goes on in a measurement; such a hypothesis is known as an interpretation of quantum mechanics. But the problem of finding a satisfactory interpretation of quantum mechanics has proven surprisingly intractable, and certainly at present there exists no single interpretation which could be regarded as a consensus view.

It should be noted that some practising physicists feel that the measurement problem is not of great importance, arguing that all interpretations of quantum mechanics make the same predictions and therefore it is not the job of physicists to decide between them. We discussed in Section 1.1 why it may be a mistake to neglect foundational questions in this way, but we must also take issue with the contention that all interpretations of quantum mechanics make the same predictions. The name 'interpretation' is misleading in this regard, because many interpretations of quantum mechanics are not really interpretations at all: they are specific hypotheses about real physical mechanisms in the world, and thus it is likely that with sufficient ingenuity and experimental sophistication we will one day be able to find ways to distinguish experimentally between them.[21] For example, we will see in Section 5.5.3 that novel predictions have already been made by proponents of the de Broglie-Bohm interpretation, although there is not yet sufficient evidence to verify (or falsify) these predictions. Furthermore, it may well be the case that some particular interpretation of quantum mechanics will one day lead us to come up with a successor theory to quantum mechanics which itself makes novel empirical predictions, and finding empirical confirmation for such a successor theory would surely count as a kind of indirect confirmation for the interpretation that prompted it.

---

[21] That said, there are some 'interpretations' which do indeed seem to be interpretations rather than physical hypotheses – for example, the Copenhagen Interpretation (Faye 2019) and Quantum Bayesianism (Fuchs 2010), which we will not cover in detail here, seem to fall into this category. It might be argued that the Everett interpretation belongs to the same class, but the Everett approach does at least make a concrete assertion about the nature of reality and there have been gestures made towards the possibility of empirical tests for it (Deutsch 2011, Barrau 2014), though it is not clear that such tests could ever be conclusive.

5.3 The Reality of the Quantum State

It is useful to distinguish two broad categories of interpretations of quantum mechanics. First, we have ψ-*ontic* views, which take the quantum state to be an element of reality, and second, ψ-*epistemic* views, which regard the quantum state as merely representing a probability distribution over some sort of underlying hidden variables. This distinction can be made precise within the ontological models picture, where it is usual to say that the quantum state is an element of reality according to a given ontological model if and only if in that model there exists no ontic state λ which is compatible with two different quantum states – that is, it is not the case that for some ontic state λ and for two different quantum states ψ, ψ', a system which is in quantum state ψ might be in the state λ but a system which is in quantum state ψ' might also be in the state λ (Harrigan and Spekkens 2010). This definition makes sense, as if every possible quantum state is associated with its own set of ontic states and these sets never overlap, then quantum states definitely represent something real in the world and are not just a description of our beliefs about ontic states.

ψ-ontic approaches may be further divided into ψ-complete models, where the quantum state is the *only* fundamental reality and everything else in the world is somehow derived from it, and ψ-supplemented models, where the quantum state is an element of reality but there are also some other hidden variables which are equally real. In the ontological models picture, a ψ-complete model would identify the ontic state with the quantum state, and a ψ-complete model would identify the ontic state with the quantum state together with some additional information (Harrigan and Spekkens 2010).

The ψ-ontic approach may initially seem very natural, as it is tempting to imagine the wavefunction as a field defined over spacetime just like an electromagnetic field. However, things are a little more complex than this, because the wavefunction is not defined on physical spacetime – it lives in *configuration space*. That is to say, the wavefunction of an n-particle system is defined on a $3n$-dimensional space, every point of which corresponds to some possible configuration of the n particles in ordinary spacetime (Chen 2019). Thus naive realism about the wavefunction would seem to entail that configuration space is the fundamental reality and four-dimensional spacetime is emergent from this underlying reality, which makes the ψ-ontic approach rather less natural. Moreover, this approach is likely to become problematic when we move to quantum field theory, since in QFT particles are not fundamental and their positions are not precisely defined, so the configuration space representation is no longer available.

Conversely, the ψ-epistemic approach may initially seem rather counterintuitive – after all, when we ascribe a state to a system in classical physics we take ourselves to be describing the way things really are in the world, and it is natural to suppose that the quantum states are similar. But ψ-epistemic approaches have a number of very attractive features: perhaps most importantly, if the quantum state is not a real physical entity then wavefunction collapse is not a real physical process, and this makes the measurement problem significantly more tractable. Usually, this idea is cashed out by claiming that the wavefunction represents an observer's beliefs or knowledge about a quantum system, and therefore in a 'wavefunction collapse' all that happens is that the observer updates their beliefs based on the measurement result (Leifer 2014) – wavefunction collapse is really nothing more than good old Bayesian updating (Stone 2013). Furthermore, it has been shown by Spekkens that ψ-epistemic models can provide convincing explanations for some of the puzzling features of quantum mechanics. Spekkens (2007) sets out a toy model for a two-dimensional quantum system, featuring four possible ontic states and an epistemic restriction requiring that we can only ever have half of the information required to specify the ontic state, so for example if we know the x-coordinate of the state we can never know the y-coordinate. Spekkens demonstrates that this simple model is able to reproduce a number of features of quantum mechanics, such as the indistinguishability of non-orthogonal pure states, the no-cloning theorem,[22] and the fact that that mixed states in quantum theory have more than one decomposition into a convex sum of pure states. Generalisations of this toy model have been put forward for larger dimensions (Schreiber and Spekkens 2008), and it has been shown that for odd dimensions, the generalised Spekkens toy model perfectly reproduces the stabilizer segment of quantum mechanics (see Section 4.5) (Leifer 2014). However, as yet there exists no epistemic model of this type which can reproduce all of quantum theory.

5.4 The PBR Theorem

The debate between ψ-ontologists and ψ-epistemicists was given new life by a recent theorem due to Pusey, Barrett, and Rudolph which has become known as the PBR Theorem (Pusey et al. 2012). In this theorem, it is shown that for any two quantum states ψ_0 and ψ_1, if we have a sufficiently large collection of quantum systems all prepared in either state ψ_0 or ψ_1, then there exists a measurement such that each outcome has probability zero for some possible combination of the states ψ_0 and ψ_1. But if there were some probability of

---

[22] The no-cloning theorem states that given a single copy of an unknown pure quantum state, we can never perform an operation which with certainty produces two perfect copies of the original state.

producing the same ontic state λ when either ψ_0 or ψ_1 were prepared, then in some cases the measuring devices would not be able to tell which set of states had been prepared, so there would be some possibility of obtaining an outcome which, according to quantum mechanics, has probability 0. This means that in an ontological model which correctly reproduces the empirical results of quantum mechanics there can never be two quantum states ψ_0, ψ_1 which are compatible with the same ontic state, and therefore the quantum state is an element of reality according to the ontological models definition.

This result was hailed in some quarters as a conclusive argument for the psi-ontic approach (Reich 2011), but others have raised objections (Leifer 2014). Particular criticism has been directed at one of the assumptions necessary to prove the PBR theorem – the Preparation Independence postulate, which states that the ontic state for two systems prepared separately can be written as the product of two separate ontic states. This postulate does seem quite plausible, since we tend to think that if two systems are prepared separately they should not have global properties that cannot be reduced to local properties of the individual systems. However, Emerson, Serbin, Sutherland, and Veitch (Emerson et al. 2013) argue that this assumption is not justified by the empirical facts, since they have come up with a way to construct models where independently prepared systems do indeed have such global properties but the global properties do not interfere with local experiments. They put forward an explicit ψ-epistemic model which has such global properties and show that this model is able to circumvent the PBR theorem, meaning that if we are willing to believe in the existence of such special global properties we are not forced to accept the conclusion of the PBR theorem.

Furthermore, note that that the PBR theorem was proved in the context of the ontological models approach, and therefore it builds in from the start the assumption that measurement results can depend on preparation procedures only via information carried forward by some mediating state, i.e. the assumption of temporal locality. Thus what the PBR theorem proves is that *if* the world is temporally local, the information carried forward in time by that mediating state must be all the same information contained in the quantum wavefunction. The theorem does not, for example, rule out the possibility that there *is* no mediating state, and instead the measuring device can tell which preparation has been performed via a direct, temporally non-local influence between the preparation and the measurement. In other words, although the PBR theorem does prove that it is necessary to have all the information present in the wavefunction in order to accurately reproduce the predictions of quantum mechanics, of course it cannot tell us that this information must necessarily be carried forwards in time by a mediating state.

This observation offers a hint to a way in which the dispute between ψ-epistemicists and ψ-ontologists might ultimately be resolved. The ψ-epistemicists want to say that the wavefunction is just a summary of our beliefs in order that wavefunction collapse can be understood as merely a process of belief-updating; the ψ-ontologists rejoinder that measurement results must depend on something real, and therefore the wavefunction must be real. But most people would accept that the past is real – so why not let measurement results be determined directly by the past in a temporally non-local fashion, without any mediating state? Thus the ψ-epistemicists get their way, since wavefunction collapse turns out to be just a process of updating our beliefs about what the future will look like based on what we know about the past, but proponents of the ψ-ontic view also get their way, since measurement results are determined by something real – the past. So it may be that we have been offered a false dilemma: perhaps in the end we will not really have to make a choice between the ψ-ontic and ψ-epistemic pictures after all.

5.5 Interpretations of Quantum Mechanics

Let us now pass to a discussion of three particularly significant approaches to the interpretation of quantum mechanics. Far more interpretations have been proposed than we could possibly cover in these pages, but the three discussed below are particularly prominent and have been developed to a high degree of sophistication.[23]

5.5.1 Spontaneous Collapse Models

One popular class of interpretations are known as spontaneous collapse models. The motivating idea is to remove the problematic category of 'measurement' from our physical laws by postulating that wavefunction collapse is a spontaneous process that occurs in quantum systems everywhere, regardless of whether or not they are being measured (Ghirardi et al. 1986a). For example, in the GRW model, systems are subject to localisations around specific positions. The localisations occur at randomly distributed times according to a Poisson distribution with mean frequency f. For a collection of n particles, a localisation of particle i at position x is modelled by acting on the n-particle

---

[23] Superdeterminism and retrocausality, which we discussed in Sections 3.3.1 and 3.3.3, are sometimes also regarded as 'interpretations' of quantum mechanics, although arguably they are better thought of as properties which interpretations might have – for example, the two-state vector formalism is a specific example of a retrocausal interpretation (Aharonov and Gruss 2005).

wavefunction with a collapse operator given by a normalised Gaussian function centered around the location x:

$$\Lambda_i(x) = \frac{1}{(2\pi\sigma^2)^{3/2}} exp[-\frac{1}{2\sigma^2}(Q_i - x)^2] \tag{5.1}$$

Here, Q_i is the position operator for particle i and σ is a parameter controlling how tightly the resulting wavefunction is localised about x. After being acted on by this operator, the wavefunction is strongly concentrated about position x – i.e. the system is now effectively localised at a unique position, so it is no longer in a spatial superposition.

The probability distribution for the location of the collapse X_i of particle i is given by the expectation value of the collapse operator:

$$p(X_i \in dx_1) = \langle\psi|\Lambda_i(x)|\psi\rangle dx_1 \tag{5.2}$$

Here, ψ is the n-particle wavefunction immediately prior to the collapse. This equation has the consequence that localisations occur with higher probability at those places where, according to the standard quantum formalism, the particle is more likely to be found if a measurement is performed.

Now the key observation for the collapse approach is that macroscopic objects such as people and measuring devices are made of enormously large numbers of entangled particles, and it follows from standard quantum mechanics that if the wavefunction of one particle spontaneously collapses, the wavefunctions of all particles entangled with it will also collapse. So as long as f is sufficiently large, for any macroscopic object and any given interval of time, the probability that at least one of its particles will undergo a wavefunction collapse in that time is very close to 1, meaning that macroscopic objects are effectively guaranteed to be in single definite states at all times. But individual quantum particles or small collections of quantum particles can still be in superposition states for long periods of time, and therefore we are still able to observe quantum phenomena which result from the existence of superposition states for microscopic particles (Ghirardi et al. 1986a, Bell 2004). We can adjust the parameters of the model to ensure that macroscopic systems are found in definite states with a high degree of certainty, while small collections of particles are still able to exist in superposition states – the values suggested in (Ghirardi et al. 1986a) are $f = 10^{-16}s^{-1}$ and $\sigma = 10^{-7}m$, which means that a macroscopic system undergoes a collapse on average every 10^{-7} seconds, but a single microscopic system will only collapse on average every hundred million years! Specific experimental results may place further constraints on these parameters, and discussion of the appropriate values for them is ongoing (Adler 2006; Toroš and Bassi 2018).

One possible difficulty for collapse theories is the 'problem of tails' (Shimony 1990). This arises because if the wavefunction collapse is expressed mathematically by an expression like 5.1, it follows that after a collapse the wavefunction will be very strongly peaked around some specific location but will nonetheless be non-zero everywhere else too. Thus the collapse alone is not enough to give us the definite macroscopic world that we are looking for – we need to add some specification of what it means in wavefunction terms for an object to have a definite macroscopic location. One proposal, known as the 'fuzzy link', says that an object is located in a particular region of configuration space as long as enough of its wavefunction is located in that region; but due to the way that configuration space grows for composite objects, this has the unfortunate consequence that we could come across a set of n marbles such that each individual marble is in a particular box but the full set of n marbles is *not* in the box, which seems in defiance of common sense. An alternative proposal is the mass-density link, where we associate the wavefunction with a mass-density over spacetime, then say that the object is in a region if it has a sufficiently high mass density over that region. This proposal gets rid of the difficulty with composite objects and thus seems a more satisfactory answer to the problem of tails, although it may be subject to other objections (Lewis 2004).

The mass-density proposal also offers one possible way of thinking about the ontology of the GRW approach: we suppose that in addition to a wavefunction there also exists a continuous field of matter over spacetime, whose density at a given point is obtained by integrating over the absolute value of the n-particle wavefunction in the following way:

$$m(x, t) = \sum_{i=1}^{n} m_i \int dq_1 ... dq_n \delta(x - x_i) |\psi_t(q_1 ... q_n, t)|^2 \qquad (5.3)$$

Here, m_i is the mass of particle i, q_i is the position of particle i, and $\psi_t(x_1 ... x_n, t)$ is the n-particle wavefunction at time. (Allori et al. 2008). Alternatively, we could take it that the wavefunction is the only fundamentally real thing and everything else in the universe supervenes on it, making the model ψ-ontic and ψ-complete.

However, both of these proposals are subject to a major problem: they appear to be inconsistent with relativity, since the wavefunction collapses everywhere instantaneously and this requires us to define a preferred reference frame for it to collapse on (Ghirardi et al. 1986b). Thus a promising alternative approach makes the spontaneous collapse theory compatible with relativity by getting rid of the wavefunction altogether and moving to an ontology which consists entirely of the collapse events, sometimes known as 'flashes'. This idea, originally proposed by Bell (2004), was developed in detail by Tumulka (2006). In this Lorentz invariant version of the theory for n non-interacting particles, we take as initial data one flash for each particle and a wavefunction obeying the Dirac equation, and then the theory defines a probability distribution for the locations of the next n flashes (one for each particle) and a prescription for determining a new wavefunction based on the location of these flashes. So we can generate a set of flashes by choosing at random from the correct distribution, updating the wavefunction, and then continuing to iterate this procedure to obtain a random series of flashes for each particle. A version for interacting particles was subsequently given in ref (Tumulka 2020).

The reason that the flash ontology solves the problem with relativity is that the flashes occur only at individual spacetime points and thus we no longer have a spatially extended wavefunction which must collapse in some particular reference frame. But there is an important caveat: as Gisin and Esfeld have observed (Esfeld and Gisin 2013), Tumulka's GRW flash model is not consistent with relativity if we insist on a causal account where the flashes that have happened in the past influence which flashes occur in the future, because changing reference frames will change the temporal ordering of the flashes and thus no such causal account can be consistent across different reference frames. Therefore we can achieve the desired reconciliation with relativity only by 'renouncing an account of the coming into being of the actual distribution of the flashes' and instead 'considering possible entire distributions of flashes'. That is, in order to achieve reconciliation with relativity we are forced to move to a global, temporally non-local approach, which is of course to be expected given the discussion in Section 3.3.2 about the impossibility of having both spatial non-locality and temporal locality in a relativistic context.

Since we arrived at the GRW flash approach by removing the wavefunction from our ontology, one might expect that this would automatically be a ψ-epistemic approach: in this picture, reality is simply composed of 'a constellation of flashes' (Bell and Aspect 2004), as Bell poetically put it. However, it should be noted that if one tried to express the GRW flash model in the ontological models framework, the ontic state would have to include the quantum state, because the quantum state is used to calculate the probabilities for the flashes. So the standard ontological models definition of the ψ-ontic/ψ-epistemic distinction (Harrigan and Spekkens 2010) would have us say that the flash approach is ψ-ontic, even though this is explicitly a picture in which the wavefunction is not part of the ontology. This apparent disagreement arises from the fact that the definitions of ψ-ontic/ψ-epistemic within the ontological models framework assume that the past can influence the future only via the mediation of ontic states, and therefore these definitions are not straight-forwardly applicable in contexts such as the flash model where, if we follow Gisin and Esfeld, we must take it that events at one time can directly influence events at other times without the relationship being mediated by a state. In such a context, we might be well-advised to replace the ψ-ontic ψ-epistemic classification with the category of 'primitive ontology' – that is to say, the 'stuff' on which the physical world of our experience is supposed to supervene (Allori et al. 2008). In the GRW flash picture, there is certainly a sense in which the wavefunction is real, since it is the wavefunction which determines the distribution of flashes, but the ordinary physical objects of our experience supervene directly on the flashes and not on the wavefunction, so the wavefunction is not a part of the primitive ontology.

5.5.2 The Everett Interpretation

The Everett interpretation is in some ways the exact opposite of the GRW flash model, since Hugh Everett's proposal was that we should simply get rid of wavefunction collapse and retain only the well-understood mechanism of the wavefunction's temporal evolution (Everett 1957). The basic equations of the Everett approach are therefore just the usual equations of unitary quantum mechanics (i.e. quantum mechanics without wavefunction collapse) (Wallace 2012).

The Everett interpretation has the advantage of simplicity, but the apparent disadvantage that if the wavefunction does not collapse then the branches associated with all the possible results of a measurement persist even after the measurement has occurred, so the theory predicts that *all* measurement outcomes will always occur! But Everett had a straightforward response to this: indeed, all measurement outcomes do always occur, but to an observer it will seem as though only one outcome occurs, because there are different observers in different branches of the wave-function and each one of them sees a different but singular outcome. The Everett interpretation is thus sometimes referred to as the 'many-worlds' interpretation, since it is as if the world branches into multiple different worlds every time a quantum measurement is performed – though this terminology is a little misleading, because all the 'worlds' are branches of a single quantum wavefunction and so, in some sense, they all belong to a single world (Wallace 2012).

As for the GRW approach, there are several proposals for how we ought to think about the ontology of the Everett interpretation. The simplest option is to say that the primitive ontology includes only the wavefunction itself (making the model ψ-ontic and ψ-complete). Adherents of this approach argue that the wavefunction alone is already capable of accounting for our empirical experience and therefore adding anything else to the ontology is an unnecessary complication. However, there remain open questions about how to recover the ordinary world of our experience from this very abstract picture (Chen 2019). Alternatively, there is also a mass-density version of the Everett interpretation, defined similarly to the mass-density version of GRW: we suppose the primitive ontology consists of a continuous distribution of matter over spacetime, and for an n-particle system, the density of matter at a point is obtained by integrating over the absolute value of the n-particle wavefunction in configuration space:

$$m(x,t) = \sum_{i=1}^{n} m_i \int dq_1...dq_n \delta(x - x_i)|\psi_t(q_1...q_n, t)|^2 \qquad (5.4)$$

Here, m_i is the mass of particle i, q_i is the position of particle i, and $\psi_t(x_1...x_n, t)$ is the n-particle wavefunction at time t. Note that unlike in the GRW version of the mass-density picture, the Everettian wavefunction never collapses and therefore we will end up with distinct, non-interacting 'branches' of the mass density, each containing different observers who are aware only of the branch that they occupy.

Perhaps the biggest problem for the Everett approach is the question of how to make sense of the probabilistic predictions of quantum theory. The idea that each observer only sees the outcome in their own branch explains why we only observe one measurement outcome, but does not say anything about why we see some particular outcome or sequence of outcomes rather than any other (Greaves 2007). This is problematic because we derive and confirm our scientific theories by performing sequences of measurements and assuming that the sequence of outcomes we observe tells us something about the underlying theory that gave rise to those outcomes – that is, we suppose that the observed sequence is highly probable according to the laws of the theory, so we can draw conclusions about those laws based on the observed relative frequencies. But Everettian quantum mechanics predicts that all possible sequences of outcomes do actually occur, so there is no straightforward way to make sense of the claim that the sequence we have seen is highly probable according to the laws of the theory, and thus it seems that in such a world *no* scientific theory could ever be regarded as empirically confirmed. So if we believe the world is Everettian we should not believe that quantum mechanics itself has any empirical confirmation! But the idea that the world is Everettian is derived from the assumption that quantum mechanics is a correct theory, and so it appears that this way of thinking about quantum mechanics is self-undermining (Kent 2009, Adlam 2014).

A more formal way of putting this argument uses the fact that observing a measurement outcome in an Everettian universe is usually regarded as giving us only *self-locating* information – that is, information about where we are in the world rather than new information about the world as a whole (Vaidman 1998, Sebens and Carroll 2016). After all, we already knew prior to the measurement that every outcome would occur and that there would be a version of us observing each outcome. Moreover, many accounts of rational belief-updating uphold the *relevance-limiting thesis*, which states that learning self-locating information should not cause us to update any non-self-locating beliefs, because we have not learned anything we did not already know about the world as a whole (Halpern and Tuttle 1993, Meacham 2008, Titelbaum 2008). If this thesis is accepted, it follows that self-locating information can not ever serve as empirical confirmation for a scientific theory (since empirical confirmation is supposed to give us grounds to update our non-self-locating beliefs about the laws of nature), and therefore in an Everettian world, measurement results could not possibly serve as empirical confirmation for a scientific theory (Adlam 2014).

To get around this objection, the Everettian needs to propose a way in which probabilities for measurement outcomes can be made meaningful even in a world in which all possible outcomes occur. One common suggestion is that these probabilities can be understood as the probabilities for the observer to end up in a particular branch, witnessing some particular outcome. But this is not really feasible, because in fact the observer ends up in all of the branches – before the measurement there is one observer, afterwards there is a plurality of observers, and there is no fact of the matter about which single post-measurement observer corresponds to the pre-measurement observer (Wallace 2012).

A more sophisticated approach is advocated by the Oxford-school Everettians led by David Deutsch and David Wallace, who have proposed a decision-theoretic approach to Everettian probabilities (Wallace 2012, Deutsch 2016). This method takes inspiration from decision theory, where there is a representation theorem showing that if an agent's preferences satisfy certain constraints of rationality (for example, an agent who prefers option A to option B and option B to option C should also prefer option A to option C), then we can define a utility function describing how much value they attach to the possible outcomes of their actions, and a credence function describing how likely they judge the possible outcomes of their actions to be, such that the agent always behaves as if they are choosing the course of action which maximises the expected utility of their outcomes according to this utility function and credence function. Classical decision theory says nothing about what these utility and credence functions should be, since this is understood to be a matter of agents' personal preference.

Deutsch and Wallace apply this idea in the quantum context and take it one step further: they demonstrate that if a person in an Everettian world has preferences which satisfy an expanded set of rationality constraints, their behaviour can be modelled mathematically using a utility function and a credence function, *and* that their credences will necessarily be equal to the values derived from the quantum mechanical Born-rule. This is supposed to prove that any rational person in an Everettian world would adopt the Born rule values as their credences. Then if we accept the famous 'Principal Principle' due to Lewis, which states that probabilities are just those things which play the role of credences in the behaviour of rational agents (Lewis 1980), it follows that the Born rule values *are* probabilities, so we have found a way to define meaningful probabilities for measurement outcomes even in this world where all outcomes occur.

This result is undoubtedly very ingenious, but there is still a great deal of debate around whether it succeeds in solving the Everettian probability problem. One concern is that the 'rationality constraints' imposed as part of the proof do not seem rationally compelling to everyone. In particular, the constraints assume that a rational agent cares only about events occurring in individual branches of the wavefunction and has no interest in the form taken by the global wavefunction containing all the branches – but given that this global wavefunction is part of the ontology of the Everett interpretation, agents surely have a right to care about it, just as they have a right to care about anything else in the world. It is true that only in-branch facts can directly affect an agent's experience, but surely we are not constrained by rationality to care only about things that directly affect us? Surely selfishness is not prescribed by rationality (Price 2008)? Similarly, Albert argues that there cannot be a uniquely rational way of assigning preferences, because we can always come up with alternatives – for example, perhaps an agent might care more about branches where their future selves are fatter, because there is more of them to be concerned about on those branches! This may sound odd but it is not actually incoherent, and therefore, Albert argues, it cannot be the case that agents in an universe are rationally compelled to organise their preferences in the way that Deutsch and Wallace suggest (Albert 2010).

A further problem is that it is not clear the decision-theoretic probabilities are the right kind of probabilities to be used in theory confirmation. For even if we grant that the decision-theoretic argument *does* prove that it is rational for agents in an Everettian universe to behave as if the Born rule values are probabilities, and thus that it is rational for Everettian agents who have seen the same sequence of measurement results as we have to behave as if they believe that quantum mechanics is correct, this does not imply that quantum mechanics *is* correct or likely to be correct. After all, there are agents in other branches of the universe who have seen other series of measurement results and who have behaved equally rationally in forming completely different beliefs – the decision theoretic argument has done nothing to reassure us that we are the agents in the branch of the world which happens to contain the 'right' sequence of results to get at the correct underlying theory. To reinforce this, Kent gives a simple example of a toy world where the preference-based probabilities over sequences of outcomes defined by the Deutsch-Wallace method are different from the 'true' probabilities defined by the number of agents who see various sequences, arguing that in such a world the Deutsch-Wallace probabilities would lead the inhabitants to confirm the wrong theories (Kent 2010). So there are still significant concerns about whether the decision-theoretic probabilities can solve the problem of confirmation, and this remains one of the key challenges for proponents of the Everett interpretation.

5.5.3 The de-Broglie-Bohm Interpretation

The final approach we will consider in detail is the de Broglie-Bohm theory. This interpretation is in some ways akin to the Everettian one – it is likewise ψ-ontic, and it likewise denies that wavefunction collapse is a real process. However, the de-Broglie Bohm approach is ψ-supplemented, as in addition to the wavefunction it postulates a set of n particles which are guided through spacetime by the wavefunction, according to the following 'guidance equation':

$$\frac{dq_k}{dt} = \frac{\hbar}{m_k} Im(\frac{\nabla_k \psi}{\psi})(q_1, q_2...q_n) \tag{5.5}$$

Here, q_k is the position of particle k, m_k is the mass of particle k, $\hbar$ is Planck's constant divided by 2π, and ψ is the usual quantum mechanical n-particle wavefunction, which evolves as usual according to the Schrödinger equation. This is the simplest first-order evolution equation for the positions of the particles that is compatible with the Galilean and time-reversal covariance of the Schrödinger equation (Durr et al. 1992).

The motivating idea here is that it is the positions of the *particles* which we find out about during quantum measurements, and thus measurements always have a single definite outcome since the de Broglie-Bohm particles cannot be in superpositions, though their paths are influenced by all the branches of the wavefunction and there is never any wavefunction collapse (Holland 1995).

The feasibility of this interpretation rests on the ingenious observation that although we can make quantum measurements of all sorts of different quantities – charge, spin, and so on – in the end, every measurement finishes with some observer making a note of the position of an indicator on a dial (or some other more complicated display) and therefore, in the end, every quantum measurement is a measurement of position. Thus in order for us to have a definite measurement result, it is enough that the de Broglie Bohm particles have a definite position.

In order to understand why an appearance of wavefunction collapse can emerge from this picture despite the fact that the de Broglie-Bohm wavefunction never collapses, it is helpful to define the *conditional* wavefunction of a quantum system. Note that the Bohmian approach postulates there is just one universal wavefunction, so Bohmian mechanics will be applicable to subsystems of the universe only when we can define a subsystem wavefunction which can be considered approximately isolated from the rest of the universal wavefunction. To do so, let us first divide all the de Broglie-Bohm particles in the universe into the set X of particles associated with the system S, and the set Y consisting of all the other particles. Let the conditional wavefunction of S at a given time be given by the wavefunction of the entire universe conditioned on the actual configuration of the particles in Y at that time. Now, the conditional wavefunction will not in general evolve according to Schrödinger's equation. But in special cases where the universal wavefunction can be written in the form $\Psi_u = \psi_S(x)\phi_{\neg S}(y) + \Psi^{\perp}(x,y)$, where $\phi_{\neg S}(y)$ and $\Psi^{\perp}(x,y)$ are associated with macroscopically distinct states of the universe, and the actual configuration of the particles in Y belongs to the support of $\phi_{\neg S}(y)$, then $\psi_S(x)$ is equal to the conditional wavefunction of S and it will evolve according to Schrödinger's equation while the system is suitably isolated. In particular, immediately after a measurement of S it is clear that the system will always be in this special form, where the macroscopically distinct states in question correspond to the possible outcomes of the measurement and $\phi_{\neg S}(y)$ is associated with the outcome which actually occurs. Thus, after the measurement, the effective wavefunction $\psi_S(x)$ is automatically equal to the wavefunction associated with the measurement outcome which has just occurred – that is, the effective wavefunction has 'collapsed' even though there is no actual collapse in the universal wavefunction (Dürr et al. 2004).

It should be noted that de Broglie-Bohm approach, like the spontaneous collapse approaches, has serious difficulties with relativity. This is because the guiding equation of de Broglie-Bohm theory tells us that when we have a collection of de Broglie-Bohm particles, the velocity of any one of the particles at a given time depends on the value of the full multi-particle wavefunction at that time; and if the particles are spread out in space, in order to define their collective wavefunction we have to be able to say what counts as 'the same time' for all these spatially separated points. But relativity, of course, tells us there is no fact of the matter about simultaneity for spatially separated points, so it looks as if the relativistic version of the de Broglie-Bohm theory will not be well-defined. A number of proposals have been made to get around this difficulty – for example, we can simply add in a preferred reference frame in which to define what counts as 'the same time', avoiding conflict with relativity by making the preferred reference frame undetectable. One might object that this seems a little arbitrary and sits poorly with the relativist denial of absolute space, but Dürr et al. (2014) shows how to extract a preferred reference frame in a covariant way from the wavefunction itself; this Machian move[24] allows us to have a preferred reference frame without the need for absolute space, making the approach more compatible with relativistic thinking. An alternative is to follow the lead of the GRW flash picture and declare that only the particles are part of the primitive ontology – the wavefunction is to be understood as a nomic feature of the universe which governs the behaviour of the particles without actually being a physical entity in and of itself (Dürr et al. 1995, Goldstein and Teufel 1999). This obviates us of the need to identify a preferred reference frame since the different definitions of 'at the same time' do not affect the behaviour of the particles and therefore these different choices can be regarded as merely a redundancy of the mathematical representation.

A further difficulty for the de Broglie-Bohm approach concerns the dual role played by the wavefunction. We have seen that the wavefunction acts as a guiding field for the de Broglie-Bohm particles, but in order for this prescription to produce results which align with standard quantum mechanics, it is also necessary that at the start of any experiment the probability distribution over various possible spacetime configurations of the de Broglie-Bohm particles is equal to the distribution given by taking the squared absolute value of the wavefunction at each point in configuration space. This seems suspiciously coincidental, since prima facie there is no reason that the guiding field and the spacetime probability distribution could not be completely independent (Dürr et al. 1995). However, there is a possible answer to this objection, arising from the observation that the quantum mechanical evolution laws have the property of equivariance – that is to say, if the spacetime probability distribution matches the magnitude of the wavefunction at some time, then it will also match the magnitude of the wavefunction at all future times. Using equivariance, it is

---

possible to show that for nearly all initial distributions of the de Broglie-Bohm particles, as temporal evolution goes on the particles will naturally move closer and closer to the wavefunction magnitude distribution, and by the present time, their distribution will be sufficiently close to it as to be indistinguishable (Durr et al. 1992). An alternative approach employs an analogue of the Boltzmann H-theorem to suggest that quantum probabilities arise dynamically in a similar way to thermal probabilities in ordinary statistical mechanics (Valentini and Westman 2005).

Using this sort of account there is no conspiracy required to get the de Broglie-Bohm particles in the right places, as they will naturally move to the wavefunction magnitude distribution, even if they were distributed very differently at the start of time. Furthermore, these proposals are quite exciting, because if they are correct, there might exist empirical evidence for them – for example, cosmologists might be able to find signs that quantum processes in the early universe did not quite conform to the same laws that we observe today, due to the de Broglie-Bohm particles not yet having reached the wavefunction magnitude distribution (Valentini 2010). Thus the de Broglie Bohm interpretation can claim to make empirical predictions which might distinguish it from other interpretations, in contradiction with the prevailing view that all interpretations of quantum mechanics are empirically equivalent.

6 Further Topics in Quantum Foundations

We have so far discussed three issues of particular importance in the field of quantum foundations, but of course, there are many further interesting questions addressed by the field which we are not able to cover in detail. In this section, we give a brief survey of several other branches of quantum foundations, and suggest resources which the interested reader could use to learn more.

6.1 Operational Theories

In the previous section, we discussed 'interpretations' of quantum mechanics – that is, attempts to understand quantum mechanics by proposing some underlying physical picture. Alternatively, we can take a more top-down approach: quantum mechanics can be thought of as simply one possible theory out of an ensemble of possible theories. This idea is usually parsed in the language of 'operational theories', with each theory defined as a quadruple (P, M, T, p), where P is the set of possible preparations, M is the set of possible measurements, T is the set of possible transformations, and the function $p(O|M^x, T^y, P^z)$ gives the probability of obtaining outcome O when we perform preparation P^z

followed by transformation T^y followed by measurement M^x (Abramsky and Heunen 2012). Nearly all theories can be written down in this form, since no mention is made of states, systems, particles, waves, or any other kind of unobservable object – we require only that the theory has a concept of preparation, transformation, and measurement. Thus by thinking of quantum mechanics as an operational theory we are in a position to compare it to a wide range of other theories and to ask why the world should in fact be governed by quantum mechanics, rather than some other operational theory.

The most ambitious way of answering this question is to propose a set of *postulates* – i.e. constraints on possible operational theories – and show that quantum mechanics is the only theory which obeys all of these postulates. Obviously, it will be possible to achieve this if we are an allowed an unlimited number of very specific postulates, but the hope is that it can be done using a small number of quite general postulates which have some intuitive plausibility, so that the postulates can be said to 'explain' quantum theory in some sense. Several suggestions for such postulates have been put forward – for example, Masanes and Muller have shown that quantum theory can be derived from the following five postulates (Masanes and Müller 2011):

1. In systems that carry one bit of information, each state is characterised by a finite set of outcome probabilities.
2. The state of a composite system is characterised by the statistics of measurements on the individual components.
3. All systems that effectively carry the same amount of information have equivalent state spaces.
4. Any pure state of a system can be reversibly transformed into any other.
5. In systems that carry one bit of information, all mathematically well-defined measurements are allowed by the theory.

The operational framework has also been put to other interesting uses. For example, one of the most intriguing properties of quantum entanglement is the fact that it is 'monogamous' – that is, there is a trade-off between the amount of entanglement that a given quantum system can share with other systems. In particular, if a given system A is maximally entangled with some system B, then it cannot share entanglement with any other system (Koashi and Winter 2004). The usual quantitative expression of the monogamy of entanglement employs a quantity known as *concurrence* (Coffman et al. 2000), but while concurrence is a mathematically tractable measure of entanglement, its physical interpretation is not straightforward (Toner 2009, Seevinck 2010), and therefore it has been found useful to study monogamy in a more general context by defining it in an operational way. In the operational framework, we can define monogamy in purely observational language by treating it as a constraint on the possible sets of correlations which can be obtained from measurements on distinct systems (Toner and Verstraete 2006, Toner 2009). This enables us to compare quantum monogamy to monogamy properties exhibited by other possible theories in the space of operational theories (Barrett 2007): in particular, it is known that all non-signalling theories obey a monogamy bound ensuring that if some set of measurements (A, A') and (B, B') on two fixed systems S_a, S_b are capable of jointly violating the CHSH inequality 3.1, then no set of measurements (C, C') on any other system S_c combined with the *same* set of measurements (A, A') on system S_a can violate the analogous CHSH inequality with B replaced everywhere by C (Toner 2009). We might therefore hope that monogamy in quantum theory can be fully explained by the constraints arising from no-signalling. However, using the operational framework, it can be shown that the region of tripartite correlations which can be achieved by measurements on entangled quantum systems is actually smaller than the region which can be achieved in a general theory constrained only by no-signalling (Toner and Verstraete 2006). It remains an open question as to whether some other physical principle might explain the gap between the quantum and no-signalling bounds: again, this problem is similar in form to the problem of explaining the gap between the quantum and no-signalling bounds on non-locality that we saw in Section 3.4, and the problem of explaining the gap between the quantum and exclusivity bounds on contextuality that we saw in Section 4.

6.2 Resource Theories

One intriguing recent development in quantum foundations involves thinking about properties of quantum mechanics in terms of resource theories.

To define a resource theory, we specify a set of 'free' states and a set of 'free' operations; then states which cannot be produced from the free states using the free operations are 'resource' states relative to the relevant operational restriction. For example, in the resource theory of entanglement, the free states are the separable states (the states with no entanglement), and the free operations are all those which involve only local operations and classical communication (LOCC) (Shahandeh 2019). Suppose we have two quantum systems A and B which are in a separable state and which are in different spatial locations: it turns out that the only states we can produce from this initial state using LOCC are other separable states,[25] which means that all non-separable states are a resource in this theory. Furthermore, we can use the resource states to perform

---

[25] Note that LOCC does not permit bringing the two particles together and performing joint operations on them – if such operations are permitted, then it is of course possible to produce an entangled state.

operations which are not free, as in the procedure known as entanglement swapping: if we are given a second pair of systems A', B' which are in an entangled state, each of which is co-located with one of the original pair of systems, we can perform a local measurement on A, A' and another local measurement on B, B', with the result that A' and B' are no longer entangled but A and B are now entangled (Żukowski et al. 1993).

Resource theories like this give us a mathematically precise framework in which to study some of the puzzling features of quantum mechanics. In particular, using a resource theory lets us quantify how useful a particular state is relative to a given restriction, and this leads to a meaningful way of quantifying properties of quantum states such as entanglement. For example, given a set of entangled mixed states, the resource theory of entanglement helps us determine how many of the more useful pure entangled states we can extract from these states using only LOCC. Indeed, it turns out that there are certain sorts of mixed states, known as 'bound entangled states', which are entangled but which cannot under any circumstances be used to obtain pure entangled states using only LOCC, so the resource theory is important in helping us to distinguish between mixed states that are useful and mixed states that are not useful relative to this particular operational constraint (Shahandeh 2019).

An exciting recent application of the resource theory framework is to quantum computing. In the resource theory of stabilizer computation (as discussed in Section 4.5), the stabilizer operations are the free operations, and the magic states are the resources (Veitch et al. 2014). Since magic states can only be produced by non-stabilizer operations, there is a lot of noise in the production process, meaning that we end up producing impure mixed states rather than the pure magic states that we need for quantum computation. However, these impure states can be converted to a smaller number of pure magic states using stabilizer operations, and the resource formalism enables us to pose and answer questions about this process – for example, given a number of impure mixed states, how many magic states (if any) can we produce from them using only stabilizer operations? In addition to their theoretical interest, these questions are of great practical importance for people engaged in the project of building real-world quantum computers.

6.3 The Role of the Observer

Consider the following experimental procedure. It involves four experimenters: A and B, who are in two separate labs, and C and D, who are outside the labs and can perform measurements on the two laboratories, including the experimenters A and B themselves.

1. Experimenter A performs a measurement on a quantum system S which is prepared in a state such that the measurement gives result H with probability $\frac{1}{3}$ and T with probability $\frac{2}{3}$. If the result is H, A prepares a particle P in the state $|1\rangle$, and if the result is T, A prepares P in the state $\frac{1}{\sqrt{2}}(|0\rangle + |1\rangle)$. A then sends P to experimenter B, who is in a separate lab.

2. Experimenter B performs the measurement $\{|0\rangle\langle 0|, |1\rangle\langle 1|\}$ on system P. This means that B will definitely obtain the result $|1\rangle\langle 1|$ if they have been sent a system P prepared in the state $|1\rangle$.

3. Experimenter C performs a measurement on the lab containing A, using a measurement which includes a measurement element projecting onto the state $|ok_C\rangle = \frac{1}{\sqrt{2}}(|H_H\rangle - |H_T\rangle)$, where $|H_H\rangle$ is the state of the lab if A obtained the result H to their measurement, and $|H_T\rangle$ is the state of the lab if A obtained the result T to their measurement.

4. Experimenter D performs a measurement on the lab containing B, using a measurement which includes a measurement element projecting onto the state $|ok_D\rangle = \frac{1}{\sqrt{2}}(|B_1\rangle - |B_0\rangle)$, where $|B_0\rangle$ is the state of the lab if B obtained the result $|0\rangle$ to their measurement and $|B_1\rangle$ is the state of the lab if B obtained the result $|1\rangle$ to their measurement.

Suppose now that all four experimenters analyse the experiment using standard quantum theory, thus coming up with a set of predictions. Each experimenter can also analyse the experiment from the point of view of each of their fellow experimenters, assuming that everyone else is also using quantum theory correctly. We suppose that each experimenter adds all the predictions they ascribe to their fellow experimenters to their own set of predictions – which is reasonable, since presumably everyone who correctly applies the same scientific theory to the same experiment must come up with the same (correct) predictions.

- Suppose experimenter A obtains the result T in their measurement of S, and thus sends B a particle P in the state $\frac{1}{\sqrt{2}}(|0\rangle + |1\rangle)$. If A now writes down the measurement performed by B as a unitary operation on the joint state of the particle P and the rest of the lab including B themself, the resulting state of the lab when P is in state $\frac{1}{\sqrt{2}}(|0\rangle + |1\rangle)$ is orthogonal to the vector $|ok_D\rangle$. So A concludes that experimenter D will definitely not obtain the result $|ok_D\rangle$.

- Suppose B obtains the result 0 in their measurement. They therefore infer that A has obtained the result T, since if A had obtained H, the particle would have been prepared in state $|1\rangle$ and the outcome of the measurement would then definitely have been $|1\rangle\langle 1|$. They therefore ascribe to A the prediction that experimenter D will definitely not obtain the result $|ok_D\rangle$, and therefore they add this to their own set of predictions.

- Suppose C now obtains the result $|ok_C\rangle$ in their measurement. If C now writes down the measurements performed by A and B as a unitary operation on the initial state of the particle S and the rest of the two labs including A and B themselves, the resulting state of the two labs is orthogonal to the state $|ok_C\rangle \otimes |B_1\rangle$. C therefore concludes that since they obtained the result $|ok_C\rangle$ to their measurement, B cannot have obtained result 1 to their measurement, so B must have obtained result 0 in their measurement. C will therefore ascribe to B the prediction that experimenter D will definitely not obtain the result $|ok_D\rangle$, so they will add this to their own set of predictions.

- Suppose C now tells D that they have obtained the result labelled $|ok_C\rangle$ in their measurement. Following the reasoning in the previous step, D will ascribe to C the prediction that D will definitely not obtain the result $|ok_D\rangle$, so they will add this to their own set of predictions.

This reasoning shows that if D learns that C has obtained the result $|ok_C\rangle$, D will then predict that their own measurement will certainly not have the result $|ok_D\rangle$. But if instead of following the reasoning above D carries out a full quantum-mechanical analysis of the above experiment, treating the two laboratories as quantum systems which can exist in superposition states, they will predict that it *is* possible for C to obtain outcome $|ok_C\rangle$ and D to obtain outcome $|ok_D\rangle$; so D can make two different and inconsistent predictions merely by considering the experiment from different points of view. Thus we have shown that quantum mechanics is not self-consistent.

In Section 5 we saw that observers seem to play a special role in quantum theory, since the act of performing a measurement results in a non-linear evolution which does not occur anywhere else in quantum mechanics. This special role was famously highlighted by Wigner in the form of the 'Wigner's Friend' thought-experiment (Wigner 1961), where an experimenter inside a box performs a measurement on a quantum particle initially prepared in the state $\frac{1}{\sqrt{2}}(|0\rangle + |1\rangle)$, and observes a result '0', then concludes that the system is now in the state $|0\rangle$. A second experimenter outside the box who does not know the outcome of the measurement must assign the joint system of the particle and friend the state $\frac{1}{\sqrt{2}}(|0\rangle|0_F\rangle + |1\rangle|1_F\rangle)$, where $|0_F\rangle$ is the state of the friend which corresponds to 'having observed the outcome 0' and $|1_F\rangle$ is the state corresponding to 'having observed the outcome 1'. Only when the second observer opens the box and learns the outcome of the measurement will they update the state to $|0\rangle|0_F\rangle$. Wigner argues that since the observer inside the box can report having a conscious state of knowledge that the state was $|0\rangle$ before the box was opened, we must in this case conclude that the state was $|0\rangle$ all along, but on the other hand, if the measurement had been made by an inanimate measuring device which simply recorded its result, the device could remain in a superposition until the box is opened, since it is not able to report that it was in a definite state before the opening of the box. Wigner thus argued that the wavefunction collapse must have something to do with consciousness.

This argument has a certain force – it undoubtedly shows up the existence of some confusion around the role of observers in quantum theory – but it does not lead to any obvious contradiction, since we saw in Section 5.5.2 that there's a credible approach to quantum mechanics which implies that a conscious observer may be in a superposition of two conscious states. Fifty years later, however, Frauchiger and Renner took the idea further by deriving a genuine contradiction (Frauchiger and Renner 2018). They came up with a specific experiment, involving two experimenters in boxes and two further experimenters observing from the outside, and imagined how the experimenters outside the boxes might reason if they tried to understand the experiment from the point of view of the experimenters in the boxes, and vice versa. Frauchiger and Renner showed that if everyone is assumed to apply quantum mechanics correctly, then under certain circumstances one of the outside experimenters will conclude that one of the inside experimenters must predict with certainty an opposite outcome to the one which has actually occurred. That is, if a quantum mechanical system contains an experimenter making calculations using quantum mechanics correctly, then quantum mechanics predicts that this experimenter will sometimes make the wrong predictions! This seems pretty disastrous for quantum mechanics – what sort of theory predicts that its own predictions will be wrong?

Of course, this disaster is for the moment only theoretical, because experimenters of the kind that Frauchinger and Renner describe cannot currently be performed: it is very difficult to keep more than a few particles at a time in a superposition state, and current technology certainly is not adequate to keep human beings made up of many millions of particles in superpositions. Nonetheless, from a foundational point of view, the result certainly seems concerning. That said, one might think that the criticism made by Frauchinger and Renner is not really fair, since the quantum-mechanical description of the experiment which predicts that it is possible for both C and D to obtain the outcome 0 is one which assumes that the laboratories can exist in a superposition of two measurement outcomes, but standard quantum mechanics includes the Born Rule, which tells us that the wavefunction collapses whenever a measurement is made and therefore this sort of superposition state is not physically possible. Rather than exposing a new contradiction in quantum mechanics, then, one might think that the Frauchiger-Renner result is simply a new way of stating the measurement problem: experimenters in quantum mechanics cannot be described as quantum systems, because quantum measurements are a special sort of process which cannot be modelled in the same way as the rest of quantum mechanics.

Nonetheless, Frauchinger and Renner's result has important consequences. As they point out, unitary quantum mechanics – that is, quantum mechanics without wavefunction collapse – is very frequently applied to domains outside the realm of microscopic experiments. For example, cosmologists often apply unitary quantum mechanics to calculations about black holes and the cosmic microwave background, assuming implicitly that it remains valid in these domains. But if quantum mechanics cannot be used consistently to describe observers then clearly it cannot be universally valid, so there is no obvious reason we should expect cosmology to obey unitary quantum mechanics. Of course, there might turn out to be some resolution of the measurement problem which has the consequence that unitary quantum mechanics is universally valid after all, but perhaps we should be wary of assuming universal validity so readily without any attempt at justification.

7 The Future of Quantum Foundations

As we have seen in this short and incomplete tour, the field of quantum foundations has made great advances since the time of Bell's theorem. However, there is still a surprising lack of consensus around questions like non-locality, contextuality, and the reality of the wavefunction, and one might well feel that the central mysteries of quantum mechanics remain intact and the project of interpreting it remains incomplete. Everyone working in the field will naturally have their own thoughts about the reason for this lack of progress, but we would like to make a suggestion which returns to the point made in Section 3.3.2: it seems highly unlikely that any theory which is both spatially non-local and temporally local can ever be reconciled with relativity, and so there should be a strong presumption in favour of either dispensing with spatial non-locality, for example by explicitly denying the assumption of statistical independence, or accepting temporal non-locality. We suggest that one or both of these possibilities must be taken up if quantum foundations is to make significant further progress.

Of course, some people working in the field might argue that statistical independence and temporal locality are no more than harmless simplifications. After all, the usual mathematical formulation of quantum mechanics is temporally local and upholds the assumption of statistical independence, so it might seem reasonable for us to retain these assumptions while we attempt to address the foundational problems of quantum mechanics, even if we accept that once we move to a relativistic context we will probably have to discard at least one of them. But this defence is inadequate, because temporal locality and statistical independence are so deeply woven into the way in which quantum foundations is usually done that the field's major results will take on very different meanings once these assumptions are abandoned. After all, Bell's theorem, the Kochen-Specker theorem, the Spekkens contextuality theorem, the PBR theorem, the Pusey-Leifer retrocausality theorem, and many other important results that we have not had time to cover are all derived within the ontological models framework, which presupposes temporal locality and statistical independence and which does not really make sense without those assumptions. Indeed, it is the founding principle of the ontological models approach that the result of a measurement of a quantum system depends wholly on the ontic state of the system *at the time of the measurement*, and there is no way to use the formalism without this assumption of temporal locality, since the whole purpose of this method of analysis is to understand what information must be contained in the ontic state in order to reproduce the empirical results of quantum mechanics, which will be impossible if we allow that the results of measurements may depend on something other than the ontic state. Likewise, there does not seem to be any way to use the ontological models framework without the assumption of statistical independence, since the framework is set up in such a way that any response function can be applied to any underlying state and we have no mechanism for introducing any dependence between the underlying state and the choice of response function. This means that many of the most important results of quantum foundations depend crucially on a pair of assumptions that almost certainly cannot both hold in the real world.

This problem also pervades most current work on the interpretation of quantum mechanics: for example, the de Broglie-Bohm and spontaneous collapse models in their standard forms both obey temporal locality and statistical independence, and thus, as we might expect, great difficulties have been encountered in the attempt to make them compatible with relativity. On the other hand, the GRW flash approach offers a promising example of what a temporally non-local interpretation of quantum mechanics might look like, and proves the point that when we adopt temporal as well as spatial non-locality, there is no longer any problem with relativity.[26]

Indeed, there seem to be many exciting possibilities for the future of quantum foundations once we come to grips with the assumptions that are getting in the way of progress. As we saw in Section 3, superdeterminism, retrocausality, and temporally non-local approaches have all been coming to greater prominence in the field, and it is to be hoped that these new ideas might finally lead us to solving the puzzles of quantum mechanics which have now persisted for more than a century. That said, as we saw in the discussion of the two forms of retrocausality in Section 3.3.3, it is easy for old ways of thinking to creep into these new conceptual frameworks, so care will have to be taken not to simply repeat old mistakes in a new language. New mathematical and conceptual tools will no doubt have to be developed for these brave new worlds, but no doubt much of our existing methodology will be applicable in some way – for example, since the operational framework makes no mention of states or temporal evolution, it is suitable to be used in the description of theories which are temporally non-local and/or retrocausal and/or superdeterministic: Oreshkov and Cerf (2016) have already set out a way of generalising the framework which does not depend on a predefined time or causal structure, thus giving us the mathematical resources to deal with theories that might contain indefinite causal order, causal loops or other structures that do not fit into our familiar notions of time and causality. Similarly, resource theory formulations also offer a new way of thinking about scientific theories without presupposing temporal locality or a direction of time.

Quantum foundations might also draw useful lessons from areas of physics which have attempted to face head-on the problem of uniting quantum mechanics and relativity. Quantum field theory and quantum gravity are not yet complete and consistent, so it would be premature to abandon quantum foundations altogether in favour of studying the foundations of these newer theories, but research in quantum foundations could profitably make use of some of the knowledge that has been accrued regarding the interaction of quantum mechanics with relativity. Similarly useful insights are coming out of the new field of relativistic quantum information, which studies the interplay between quantum

---

[26] It is not straightforward to say whether the Everett interpretation obeys temporal locality and/or statistical independence, since space, time and probability are so very different from our usual concepts of them in the Everettian context; it is also not straightforward to say whether or not the Everett view is compatible with relativity.

information and relativity (Kent 2013, Edward Bruschi et al. 2014, Lind-kvist et al. 2015, Bruschi et al. 2016). Putting quantum mechanics back in its real-world relativistic context might shed new light on some of the conceptual problems studied in quantum foundations, and seems a more promising approach if our aim is to understand what sort of mechanisms could underpin quantum mechanics in the actual universe in which we live.

Of course, this is only the present author's perspective on the future of quantum foundations; other researchers will have other ideas, and perhaps by this stage the reader will be drawing their own conclusions! We hope at least to have made a convincing argument that quantum foundations is important for both intellectual and practical reasons, and that many exciting directions within the field are yet to be fully explored. We encourage interested readers to explore further using the books and papers that have been referenced throughout this text.

References

Aaronson, S., and Gottesman, D. (2004). Improved simulation of stabilizer circuits. *Physical Review A*, 70:052328.

Abramsky, S., and Heunen, C. (2012). Operational theories and categorical quantum mechanics. In Logic and Algebraic Structures in Quantum Computing. Cambridge University Press.

Adlam, E. (2014). The problem of confirmation in the Everett interpretation. *Studies in History and Philosophy of Science Part B: Studies in History and Philosophy of Modern Physics*, 47:21–32.

Adlam, E. (2018a). Quantum mechanics and global determinism. *Quanta*, 7(1):40–53.

Adlam, E. (2018b). Spooky action at a temporal distance. *Entropy*, 20(1):41.

Adler, S. L. (2006). Lower and upper bounds on CSL parameters from latent image formation and IGM heating. *Journal of Physics A: Mathematical and Theoretical*, 40:2935–2957.

Aharonov, Y., Cohen, E., Gruss, E., and Landsberger, T. (2014). Measurement and collapse within the two-state vector formalism. *Quantum Studies: Mathematics and Foundations*, 1(1–2):133–146.

Aharonov, Y., and Gruss, E. Y. (2005). Two-time interpretation of quantum mechanics. *eprint arXiv:quant-ph/0507269*.

Albert, D. (2010). Probability in the Everett picture. In Saunders, S., Barrett, J., Kent, A., and Wallace, D., editors, *Many Worlds?: Everett, Quantum Theory & Reality*. Oxford University Press.

Allori, V., Goldstein, S., Tumulka, R., and Zanghì, N. (2008). On the common structure of Bohmian mechanics and the Ghirardi-Rimini-Weber theory. *British Journal for the Philosophy of Science*, 59(3):353–389.

Allori, V., Goldstein, S., Tumulka, R., and Zanghi, N. (2013). Predictions and primitive ontology in quantum foundations: A study of examples. *British Journal for the Philosophy of Science*, 65(2):323–352.

Arntzenius, F. (1994). Spacelike connections. *British Journal for the Philosophy of Science*, 45(1):201–217.

Aspect, A., Grangier, P., and Roger, G. (1981). Experimental tests of realistic local theories via Bell's theorem. *Physical Review Letters*, 47:460–463.

Barrau, A. (2014). Testing the Everett interpretation of quantum mechanics with cosmology. *Electronic Journal of Theoretical Physics*, 33:127–134.

Barrett, J. (2007). Information processing in generalized probabilistic theories. *Physical Review A*, 75:032304.

Bell, J. (1987). Free variables and local causality. In *Speakable and Unspeakable in Quantum Mechanics*. Cambridge University Press.

Bell, J. (2004). Are there quantum jumps? In *Speakable and Unspeakable in Quantum Mechanics*, 2nd edition. Cambridge University Press.

Bell, J. S. (1985). Free variables and local causality. In *John S. Bell on the Foundations of Quantum Mechanics*. World Scientific.

Bell, J. S. (1964). On the Einstein Podolsky Rosen paradox. *Physics Physique Fizika*, 1(3):195.

Bell, J. S. (1966). On the problem of hidden variables in quantum mechanics. *Reviews of Modern Physics*, 38(3):447.

Bell, J. S., and Aspect, A. (2004). Are there quantum jumps? In *Speakable and Unspeakable in Quantum Mechanics*, 2nd edition. Cambridge University Press.

Beltrametti, E., and Bujaski, S. (1995). A classical extension of quantum mechanics. *Journal of Physics A: Mathematics and General*, 37(28):3329–3343.

Berkovitz, J. (2002). On causal loops in the quantum realm. In Placek, T. and Butterfield, J., editors, *Non-locality and Modality*. Kluwer.

Black, M. (1956). Why cannot an effect precede its cause? *Analysis*, 16(3):49–58.

Bondy, J., and Murty, U. (1976). *Graph Theory with Applications*. Elsevier Science Publishing.

Bravyi, S., and Kitaev, A. (2005). Universal quantum computation with ideal Clifford gates and noisy ancillas. *Physical Review A.*, 71(2):022316.

Brizard, A. (2008). *An Introduction to Lagrangian Mechanics*. World Scientific.

Brown, H. R., and Lehmkuhl, D. (2016). Einstein, the reality of space, and the action-reaction principle. In *Einstein, Tagore and the Nature of Reality*, Routledge Studies in the Philosophy of Mathematics and Physics. Taylor & Francis.

Bruschi, D. E., Sabín, C., Kok, P., Johansson, G., Delsing, P., and Fuentes, I. (2016). Towards universal quantum computation through relativistic motion. *Scientific Reports*, 6(1):18349.

Busch, P., Lahti, J., and Mittelstaedt, P. (1996). *The Quantum Theory of Measurement*. Springer-Verlag.

Butterfield, J. (1992). Bell's theorem: What it takes. *British Journal for the Philosophy of Science*, 43(1):41–83.

Cabello, A., Estebaranz, J., and García-Alcaine, G. (1996). Bell-Kochen-Specker theorem: A proof with 18 vectors. *Physics Letters A*, 212(4):183–187.

Cabello, A., Severini, S., and Winter, A. (2014). Graph-theoretic approach to quantum correlations. *Physical Review Letters*, 112(4):040401.

Chen, E. K. (2019). Realism about the wave function. *Philosophy Compass*, 14(7):e12611.

Clauser, J. F., Horne, M. A., Shimony, A., and Holt, R. A. (1969). Proposed experiment to test local hidden-variable theories. *Physical Review Letters*, 23:880–884.

Coffman, V., Kundu, J., and Wootters, W. K. (2000). Distributed entanglement. *Physical Review A*, 61(5):052306.

Cramer, J. G. (1986). The transactional interpretation of quantum mechanics. *Reviews of Modern Physics*, 58:647–687.

Cuffaro, M. E. (2015). On the significance of the Gottesman–Knill theorem. *British Journal for the Philosophy of Science*, 68(1):91–121.

d' Espagnat, B. (1971). *Conceptual Foundations of Quantum Mechanics*. Addison-Wesley.

de Muynck, W. M. (2007). POVMs: A small but important step beyond standard quantum mechanics. In Nieuwenhuizen, T. M., Mehmani, B., Špička, V., Aghdami, M. J., and Khrennikov, A. Y., editors, *Beyond the Quantum*. World Scientific.

Deutsch, D. (2011). *The Fabric of Reality*. Penguin Books.

Deutsch, D. (2016). The logic of experimental tests, particularly of Everettian quantum theory. *Studies in History and Philosophy of Science Part B: Studies in History and Philosophy of Modern Physics*, 55:24–33.

Dürr, D., Goldstein, S., and Zanghì, N. (1992). Quantum equilibrium and the origin of absolute uncertainty. *Journal of Statistical Physics*, 67(5–6).

Dürr, D., Goldstein, S., and Zanghì, N. (1995). Bohmian mechanics and the meaning of the wave function. In *Experimental Metaphysics: Quantum Mechanical Studies in Honor of Abner Shimony*. Springer.

Dürr, D., Goldstein, S., and Zanghì, N. (2004). Quantum equilibrium and the role of operators as observables in quantum theory. *Journal of Statistical Physics*, 116(1-4):959–1055.

Dürr, D., Goldstein, S., Norsen, T., Struyve, W., and Zanghì, N. (2014). Can Bohmian mechanics be made relativistic? *Proceedings of the Royal Society A: Mathematical, Physical and Engineering Sciences*, 470(2162):20130699.

Dürr, D., Goldstein, S., Tumulka, R., and Zanghì, N. (2005). On the role of density matrices in Bohmian mechanics. *Foundations of Physics*, 35(3):449–467.

Eastin, B., and Knill, E. (2009). Restrictions on transversal encoded quantum gate sets. *Physical Review Letters*, 102(11):110502.

Edward Bruschi, D., Sabín, C., White, A., Baccetti, V., Oi, D. K. L., and Fuentes, I. (2014). Testing the effects of gravity and motion on quantum entanglement in space-based experiments. *New Journal of Physics*, 16(5):053041.

Einstein, A. (1905). On the electrodynamics of moving bodies. *Annalen der Physik*, 17:891–921.

Einstein, A. (1920). *Relativity: The Special and General Theory*. Henry Holt.

Einstein, A. (1948). Quantum mechanics and reality. *Dialectica* 2(3–4):320–324.

Einstein, A., Podolsky, B., and Rosen, N. (1935). Can quantum-mechanical description of physical reality be considered complete? *Physical Review*, 47:777–780.

Emerson, J., Serbin, D., Sutherland, C., and Veitch, V. (2013). The whole is greater than the sum of the parts: On the possibility of purely statistical interpretations of quantum theory. *ArXiv eprints*.

Esfeld, M., and Gisin, N. (2013). The GRW flash theory: A relativistic quantum ontology of matter in space-time? *ArXiv eprints*.

Everett, H. (2016). 'Relative state' formulation of quantum mechanics. In *The Many-Worlds Interpretation of Quantum Mechanics*. Princeton University Press.

Faye, J. (2019). Copenhagen interpretation of quantum mechanics. In Zalta, E. N., editor, *The Stanford Encyclopedia of Philosophy, winter 2019 edition*. Metaphysics Research Lab, Stanford University.

Frauchiger, D., and Renner, R. (2018). Quantum theory cannot consistently describe the use of itself. *Nature Communications*, 9(1):3711.

Friederich, S., and Evans, P. W. (2019). Retrocausality in quantum mechanics. In Zalta, E. N., editor, *The Stanford Encyclopedia of Philosophy, summer 2019 edition*. Metaphysics Research Lab, Stanford University.

Fuchs, C. A. (2010). QBism, the perimeter of quantum Bayesianism. *ArXiv eprints*.

Gell-Mann, M. (1980). Questions for the future. In *Wolfson College Lectures*. Oxford University Press.

Ghirardi, G. C., Rimini, A., and Weber, T. (1986a). Unified dynamics for microscopic and macroscopic systems. *Physical Review D*, 34:470–491.

Ghirardi, G. C., Rimini, A., and Weber, T. (1986b). Unified dynamics for microscopic and macroscopic systems. *Physical Review D*, 34:470–491.

Goldstein, S., and Teufel, S. (1999). Quantum spacetime without observers: Ontological clarity and the conceptual foundations of quantum gravity. In *Quantum Physics Without Quantum Philosophy*. Springer.

Goldstein, S., and Tumulka, R. (2003). Opposite arrows of time can reconcile relativity and nonlocality. *Classical and Quantum Gravity*, 20(3):557–564.

Gottesman, D. (1998). The Heisenberg representation of quantum computers. Speech at the 1998 International Conference on Group Theoretic Methods in Physics.

Greaves, H. (2007). Probability in the Everett interpretation. *Philosophy Compass*, 2(1):109–128.

Halpern, J. Y., and Tuttle, M. R. (1993). Knowledge, probability, and adversaries. *Journal of the ACM*, 40(4):917–960.

Hardy, L., and Spekkens, R. (2010). Why physics needs quantum foundations. *Physics in Canada*, 66(2):73–76.

Harrigan, N., and Spekkens, R. W. (2010). Einstein, incompleteness, and the epistemic view of quantum states. *Foundations of Physics*, 40:125–157.

Held, C. (2014). The Kochen-Specker theorem. In Zalta, E. N., editor, *The Stanford Encyclopedia of Philosophy, winter 2014 edition*. Metaphysics Research Lab, Stanford University.

Hensen, B., Bernien, H., Dréau, A. E., Reiserer, A., Kalb, N., Blok, M. S., Ruitenberg, J., Vermeulen, R. F. L., Schouten, R. N., Abellán, C., Amaya, W., Pruneri, V., Mitchell, M. W., Markham, M., Twitchen, D. J., Elkouss, D., Wehner, S., Taminiau, T. H., and Hanson, R. (2015). Experimental loophole-free violation of a Bell inequality using entangled electron spins separated by 1.3 km. *Nature*, 526:682–686.

Hesse, M. B. (1955). Action at a distance in classical physics. *Isis*, 46(4):337–353.

Hoefer, C. (2016). Causal determinism. In Zalta, E. N., editor, *The Stanford Encyclopedia of Philosophy, spring 2016 edition*. Metaphysics Research Lab, Stanford University.

Holland, P. (1995). *The Quantum Theory of Motion: An Account of the de Broglie-Bohm Causal Interpretation of Quantum Mechanics*. Cambridge University Press.

Horne, M. A., Clauser, J. F., and Shimony, A. (1993). *An Exchange on Local Beables*, volume 2. Cambridge University Press.

Hossenfelder, S. (2018). *Lost in Math: How Beauty Leads Physics Astray*. Basic Books.

Hossenfelder, S., and Palmer, T. (2020). Rethinking superdeterminism. *Frontiers in Physics*, 8:139.

Howard, M., Wallman, J., Veitch, V., and Emerson, J. (2014). Contextuality supplies the 'magic' for quantum computation. *Nature*, 510:351–355.

Kent, A. (2009). One world versus many: The inadequacy of Everettian accounts of evolution, probability, and scientific confirmation. In *Many Worlds? Everett, Quantum Theory and Reality*. Oxford University Press.

Kent, A. (2010). One world versus many: The inadequacy of Everettian accounts of evolution, probability, and scientific confirmation. In Saunders, S., Barrett, J., Kent, A., and Wallace, D., editors, *Many Worlds?: Everett, Quantum Theory & Reality*. Oxford University Press.

Kent, A. (2013). A no-summoning theorem in relativistic quantum theory. *Quantum Information Processing*, 12(2):1023–1032.

Kielpinski, D., Meyer, V., Sackett, C. A., Itano, W. M., Monroe, C., and Wineland, D. J. (2001). Experimental violation of a Bell's inequality with efficient detection. *Nature*, 409:791–794.

Koashi, M., and Winter, A. (2004). Monogamy of quantum entanglement and other correlations. *Physical Review A*, 69(2):022309.

Kochen, S., and Specker, E. (1975). The problem of hidden variables in quantum mechanics. In Hooker, C., editor, *The Logico-Algebraic Approach to Quantum Mechanics*, volume 5a of *The University of Western Ontario Series in Philosophy of Science*. Springer.

Kuhlmann, M. (2018). Quantum field theory. In Zalta, E. N., editor, *The Stanford Encyclopedia of Philosophy, winter 2018 edition*. Metaphysics Research Lab, Stanford University.

Lancaster, T., and Blundell, S. (2014). *Quantum Field Theory for the Gifted Amateur*. Oxford University Press.

Landau, L., and Lifshitz, E. (2013). *Quantum Mechanics: Non-Relativistic Theory*. Elsevier Science.

Leifer, M. (2014). Is the quantum state real? An extended review of ψ-ontology theorems. *Quanta*, 3(1):67–155.

Leifer, M., and Pusey, M. (2017). Is a time symmetric interpretation of quantum theory possible without retrocausality? *Proceedings of the Royal Society A*.

Lewis, D. K. (1980). A subjectivist's guide to objective chance. In Jeffrey, R. C., editor, *Studies in Inductive Logic and Probability*, volume 2. University of California Press.

Lewis, P. J. (2004). Interpreting spontaneous collapse theories. *Studies in History and Philosophy of Science Part B: Studies in History and Philosophy of Modern Physics*, 36(1):165–180.

Lindkvist, J., Sabín, C., Johansson, G., and Fuentes, I. (2015). Motion and gravity effects in the precision of quantum clocks. *Scientific Reports*, 5(1):10070.

Lindley, D. (2008). *Uncertainty*. Knopf Doubleday.

MacKenzie, R. (2000). Path integral methods and applications. Lectures given at Rencontres du Vietnam, 6. Vietnam School of Physics.

Mari, A., and Eisert, J. (2012). Positive Wigner functions render classical simulation of quantum computation efficient. *Physical Review Letters*, 109:230503.

Masanes, L., and Müller, M. P. (2011). A derivation of quantum theory from physical requirements. *New Journal of Physics*, 13(6):063001.

Maudlin, T. (2011). *Quantum Non-locality and Relativity: Metaphysical Intimations of Modern Physics*. Wiley.

Maudlin, T. (2012). *Philosophy of Physics: Space and Time*. Princeton University Press.

Meacham, C. J. G. (2008). Sleeping beauty and the dynamics of de se beliefs. *Philosophical Studies*, 138(2):245–269.

Navascués, M., Guryanova, Y., Hoban, M. J., and Acín, A. (2015). Almost quantum correlations. *Nature Communications*, 6(1):6288.

Nielsen, M. A., and Chuang, I. L. (2011). *Quantum Computation and Quantum Information, 10th edition*. Cambridge University Press.

Oreshkov, O., and Cerf, N. J. (2016). Operational quantum theory without predefined time. *New Journal of Physics*, 18(7):073037.

Paris, M. G. A. (2012). The modern tools of quantum mechanics. A tutorial on quantum states, measurements, and operations. *European Physical Journal Special Topics*, 203:61–86.

Pawlowski, M., Paterek, T., Kaszlikowski, D., Scarani, V., Winter, A., and Żukowski, M. (2009). Information causality as a physical principle. *Nature*, 461:1101–1104.

Peskin, M., and Schroeder, D. (1995). *An Introduction to Quantum Field Theory*. Westview Press.

Price, H. (1994). A neglected route to realism about quantum mechanics. *Mind*, 103(411):303–336.

Price, H. (2008). Decisions, decisions, decisions: Can Savage salvage Everettian probability? Presented at the Many Worlds at 50 conference. Perimeter Institute.

Price, H. (2010). Does Time-Symmetry Imply Retrocausality? How the Quantum World Says 'Maybe'. *Studies in History and Philosophy of Modern Physics*, 43:75–83.

Pusey, M. F., Barrett, J., and Rudolph, T. (2012). On the reality of the quantum state. *Nature Physics*, 8:476–479.

Robinson, H. (2017). Dualism. In Zalta, E. N., editor, *The Stanford Encyclopedia of Philosophy, fall 2017 edition*. Metaphysics Research Lab, Stanford University.

Rohrlich, D., and Popescu, S. (1995). Nonlocality as an axiom for quantum theory. Presented at 60 Years of E.P.R. conference, Israel.

Samuel Reich, E. (2011). Quantum theorem shakes foundations. *Nature.* www.nature.com/news/quantum-theorem-shakes-foundations-1.9392.

Sartori, L. (1996). *Understanding Relativity: A Simplified Approach to Einstein's Theories.* University of California Press.

Schreiber, O., and Spekkens, R. (2008). The power of epistemic restrictions in axiomatizing quantum theory: From trits to qutrits. *Unpublished work. Videos of talks discussing this material are available: Spekkens R. W., Talk, July 17, 2008, University of Oxford, Spekkens R. W., Talk, August 10, 2008, Perimeter Institute, PIRSA:09080009.*

Sebens, C. T., and Carroll, S. M. (2016). Self-locating uncertainty and the origin of probability in Everettian quantum mechanics. *British Journal for the Philosophy of Science*, 69(1):25–74.

Seevinck, M. P. (2010). Can quantum theory and special relativity peacefully coexist? In *Quantum Physics and the Nature of Reality.* Oxford University Press.

Seevinck, M. P. (2010). Monogamy of correlations versus monogamy of entanglement. *Quantum Information Processing*, 9(2):273–294.

Shahandeh, F. (2019). *The Resource Theory of Entanglement*, Springer International.

Shimony, A. (1990). Desiderata for a modified quantum dynamics. *PSA: Proceedings of the Biennial Meeting of the Philosophy of Science Association*, 1990:49–59.

Shimony, A. (2013). Bell's theorem. In Zalta, E. N., editor, *The Stanford Encyclopedia of Philosophy, winter 2013 edition.* Metaphysics Research Lab, Stanford University.

Sklar, L. (1993). *Physics and Chance: Philosophical Issues in the Foundations of Statistical Mechanics.* Cambridge University Press.

Sklar, L. (2012). *Philosophy and the Foundations of Dynamics.* Cambridge University Press.

Spekkens, R. W. (n.d.). Private communication.

Spekkens, R. W. (2005). Contextuality for preparations, transformations, and unsharp measurements. *Physical Review A*, 71(5):052108.

Spekkens, R. W. (2007). Evidence for the epistemic view of quantum states: A toy theory. *Physical Review A*, 75(3):032110.

Stone, J. (2013). *Bayes' Rule: A Tutorial Introduction to Bayesian Analysis.* Sebtel Press.

Strang, G. (2016). *Introduction to Linear Algebra.* Cambridge University Press.

Thomas, J., and Cover, T. (2006). *Elements of Information Theory.* Wiley.

Timpson, C. G. (2008). Philosophical aspects of quantum information theory. In Rickles, D., editor, *The Ashgate Companion to Contemporary Philosophy of Physics*. Ashgate.

Titelbaum, M. G. (2008). The relevance of self-locating beliefs. *The Philosophical Review*, 117(4):555–605.

Toner, B. (2009). Monogamy of non-local quantum correlations. *Proceedings of the Royal Society of London Series A*, 465:59–69.

Toner, B., and Verstraete, F. (2006). Monogamy of Bell correlations and Tsirelson's bound. *eprint arXiv:quant-ph/0611001*.

Toroš, M., and Bassi, A. (2018). Bounds on quantum collapse models from matter-wave interferometry: Calculational details. *Journal of Physics A: Mathematical and Theoretical*, 51(11):115302.

Tsirelson, B. S. (1980). Quantum generalizations of Bell's inequality. *Letters in Mathematical Physics*. 4:93–100.

Tumulka, R. (2006). A relativistic version of the Ghirardi–Rimini–Weber model. *Journal of Statistical Physics*, 125(4):821–840.

Tumulka, R. (2020). A relativistic GRW flash process with interaction. n.p.

Vaidman, L. (1998). On schizophrenic experiences of the neutron or why we should believe in the many-worlds interpretation of quantum theory. *International Studies in the Philosophy of Science*, 12(3):245–261.

Valentini, A. (2010). Inflationary cosmology as a probe of primordial quantum mechanics. *Physical Review D*, 82(6): 063513.

Valentini, A., and Westman, H. (2005). Dynamical origin of quantum probabilities. *Proceedings of the Royal Society A: Mathematical, Physical and Engineering Sciences*, 461(2053):253–272.

Veitch, V., Ferrie, C., Gross, D., and Emerson, J. (2012). Negative quasi-probability as a resource for quantum computation. *New Journal of Physics*, 14(11):113011.

Veitch, V., Hamed Mousavian, S. A., Gottesman, D., and Emerson, J. (2014). The resource theory of stabilizer quantum computation. *New Journal of Physics*, 16(1):013009.

Wallace, D. (2007). The quantum measurement problem: State of play. In *The Ashgate Companion to the New Philosophy of Physics*. Ashgate.

Wallace, D. (2012). *The Emergent Multiverse: Quantum Theory according to the Everett Interpretation*. Oxford University Press.

Walleczek, J., and Grössing, G. (2014). The non-signalling theorem in generalizations of Bell's theorem. In *Journal of Physics: Conference Series*, volume 504, page 012001. IOP Publishing.

Weinberg, S. (2014). Quantum mechanics without state vectors. *Physical Review A*, 90(4):042102.

Wharton, K. (2015). The universe is not a computer. In Aguirre, A., F. B., and Merali, G., editors, *Questioning the Foundations of Physics*. Springer.

Wigner, E. P. (1961). Remarks on the mind-body question. In Good, I. J., editor, *The Scientist Speculates*. Heineman.

Wiseman, H. M. (2006). From Einstein's theorem to Bell's theorem: A history of quantum non-locality. *Contemporary Physics*, 47:79–88.

Żukowski, M., Zeilinger, A., Horne, M. A., and Ekert, A. K. (1993). 'Event-ready-detectors' Bell experiment via entanglement swapping. *Physical Review Letters*, 71:4287–4290.

Cambridge Elements ☰

The Philosophy of Physics

James Owen Weatherall

University of California, Irvine

James Owen Weatherall is Professor of Logic and Philosophy of Science at the University of California, Irvine. He is the author, with Cailin O'Connor, of *The Misinformation Age: How False Beliefs Spread* (Yale, 2019), which was selected as a New York Times Editors' Choice and Recommended Reading by *Scientific American*. His previous books were *Void: The Strange Physics of Nothing* (Yale, 2016) and the *New York Times* bestseller *The Physics of Wall Street: A Brief History of Predicting the Unpredictable* (Houghton Mifflin Harcourt, 2013). He has published approximately fifty peer-reviewed research articles in journals in leading physics and philosophy of science journals and has delivered over 100 invited academic talks and public lectures.

About the Series

This Cambridge Elements series provides concise and structured introductions to all the central topics in the philosophy of physics. The Elements in the series are written by distinguished senior scholars and bright junior scholars with relevant expertise, producing balanced, comprehensive coverage of multiple perspectives in the philosophy of physics.

Cambridge Elements ≡

The Philosophy of Physics

Printed in the United States
By Bookmasters